TERNARY SYSTEMS

INTRODUCTION TO THE THEORY OF THREE COMPONENT SYSTEMS

By

G. MASING

Translated by

B. A. ROGERS

DOVER PUBLICATIONS, INC.

NEW YORK   NEW YORK

Library of Congress Catalog Card Number: 60-3184

Manufactured in the United States of America

Dover Publications, Inc.
180 Varick Street
New York 14, N.Y.

Preface

Although constitutional diagrams of binary systems have been described so thoroughly that it is now a simple matter to study in this field and to obtain a background which makes possible the understanding and even the construction of such diagrams, the same statement is not at all true of three-component systems. Information concerning the latter is mostly contained in a series of articles covering special cases or a group of special cases. In general textbooks which take up the discussion of heterogeneous equilibria, ternary systems are generally treated in a rather brief appendix to the section concerned with binary systems. These treatments are in all cases so short that the reader immediately encounters trouble upon attempting to proceed further. He is then forced to obtain an understanding of this field by his own efforts without the advantage of a systematic introduction, a method which is very instructive but also very laborious and costly in time. For this reason only a comparatively small number of technical workers find opportunity to delve into ternary systems sufficiently to feel at home in this field, whereas most, although they understand quite well the heterogeneous equilibria of binary systems, have difficulty in analyzing even the simplest ternary systems. Indeed, many works on ternary systems show violations of the elementary teachings regarding equilibria which indicate that the author himself is not well grounded in the theory underlying such systems.

The advance of systematic alloying science and technique demands increasing attention to the field of ternary and higher alloys. Knowledge of such alloys becomes continually more important and the need for an elementary but sound introduction to the subject for both the student and technician increases correspondingly.

The purpose of the present work is to fill this gap by a discussion of the fundamental theory underlying ternary systems.

The study of three-component systems is rightly considered to be very difficult. This condition arises not only from the greater complexity of ternary systems in comparison with the binary type but more especially because the diagrams cannot be exhibited as plane figures but require a spatial representation. For this reason, the subject sets up unusually high requirements as to clearness and thoroughness of explanation. An effort has been made to have the discussion in this treatise as concrete and informative as possible. Special care has been taken with reference to the difficulties which the beginner meets. Interruptions in the sequence of ideas have been avoided as much as possible, and care has been taken to deal fully with those mental transitions which the beginner finds troublesome. Only the simpler structural cases have been described, but those have been discussed thoroughly. It is hoped that in this way the reader will be able to learn without excessive difficulty the fundamental theory underlying ternary systems, and that with the knowledge so obtained, he will have little trouble in understanding the cases which occur in practice or in working out more complicated systems.

The methods used in investigating ternary alloy systems will receive little attention here. For one thing, such methods do not differ particularly from those used in studying binary systems and, for another, such a description is beyond the scope of this book. It appears more desirable to enliven the subject by discussing some of the more important industrial alloys. This plan has been carried out in the last three chapters.

Although the presentation has been made on the basis of metallic alloys, the conclusions are valid also for non-metallic systems as long as the vapor pressure is negligible.

The author is indebted to Dr. O. Dahl, Dr. M. Hansen, and Dr. W. Pocher, who have most kindly given the text a critical reading and eliminated numerous deficiencies of presentation, and to Dr. Ewig-Daus for reading the proofs.

Berlin-Siemensstadt
September, 1932.

G. MASING.

Contents

TERNARY SYSTEMS

INTRODUCTION TO THE THEORY OF
THREE COMPONENT SYSTEMS

Chapter I

Introduction

1. THERMODYNAMIC FUNDAMENTALS

The relationships in systems containing one or two components can be so readily understood from ordinary experience that few thermodynamic considerations need be brought into their discussion. In such systems, the phase rule, which is the most important of the thermodynamic laws relating to heterogeneous equilibria, is of secondary importance. Hence this rule has generally not been introduced in the early part of discussions of heterogeneous systems but has been relegated to an appendix.

The facts are otherwise when systems with three or more components are considered. These systems are inherently more complicated than the singular or binary types. Their temperature-concentration diagrams at constant pressure cannot be shown on a plane surface but must be represented by a space figure, a fact which makes their analysis more difficult. It is, therefore, less easy to comprehend the entire problem from a simple point of view, and for the sake of avoiding confusion, explanations should be based on formal thermodynamic laws. For this reason, the phase rule will be taken up at the beginning of this exposition of ternary systems. In making a short recapitulation of the theoretical foundation it will be assumed that the reader is familiar with the simple form of this law as applied to systems of one or two components.

In thermodynamics we recognize a distinction between homogeneous and heterogeneous systems. A homogeneous system is one in which the chemical composition and the properties—as specific volume, color, electrochemical solution potential, electrical conductivity, etc.—are the same in every part of the system. In any system—homogeneous or heterogeneous—which is in equilibrium, the temperature and pressure are the same at all points. Hence, in the case of a homogeneous system, it is possible to set up an equation of state involving a relation between temperature, pressure, composition, and the various properties, which will completely define the behavior of the system. The simplest case is that of a system of one component such as a homogeneous gas (hydrogen, oxygen, water vapor, and so on). For such a system, the equation of state is

$$f(P,T,V) = 0, \tag{1}$$

1

where P is the pressure, T the absolute temperature, and V the specific volume. For an ideal gas the function (1) takes the simple and familiar form of the gas law

$$PV=RT, \qquad (2)$$

where R is the gas constant and V the volume of a mol of gas at a given temperature and pressure. In general, particularly for liquids and solids, the equation of state is more complicated than (2); fundamentally, it is expressed by, or can be brought into the form of (1).

Experience has shown that if the equation of state of a system composed of one substance is known, it is necessary only to specify two of the three variables, *e.g.*, the pressure and the temperature, the pressure and the specific volume, or the temperature and the specific volume, in order to fix all the properties of the substance. Just as the specific volume is determined by the pressure and the temperature, so are all the other properties of the substance; and this statement holds regardless of the state of aggregation.

If the problem involves more than one constituent, as in the case of a homogeneous substance composed of two or more components, then the properties depend upon the composition as well as upon the pressure and the temperature. The composition is expressed by the relative concentrations, c, of the different constituents—that is, the ratio of their mass, m, to the total mass of the system—thus:

$$c_n=\frac{m_n}{M}, \qquad (3)$$

where the subscript n denotes that the nth constituent is under consideration. For the determination of the composition of a system containing n constituents, it is necessary that $n-1$ concentrations be specified; thus, for a three-component system, two concentrations must be specified. The concentration of the last constituent is, of course, given by subtracting the sum of the $n-1$ concentrations from the total concentration. For a homogeneous system of n components, the equation of state corresponding to (1) has the form:

$$F(c_1,c_2\ldots c_{n-1},P,T,V)=0. \qquad (4)$$

In simple cases, the validity of the above equation is at once evident. Consider, for example, the case of a homogeneous solution in a closed space. The volume and other properties of the solution are known as soon as the pressure, temperature, and $n-1$ concentrations have been fixed.

The empirical fact of the existence of an equation of state containing $n+2$ variables, as shown in (4), capable of specifying the behavior of a homogeneous body composed of n constituents, is the fundamental hypothesis upon which the phase rule rests. The importance of this equation is not set forth with sufficient clearness in most treatises dealing with this subject. That an equation of state contains exactly $n+2$ variables, and hence that a simple gas has no other independent variables than V, P, and T,* is an experimental fact with no theoretical foundation. The fundamental significance of this fact makes desirable a detailed discussion of it with respect to the phase rule.

A system which is composed of more than one homogeneous portion is said to be a heterogeneous system. The several homogeneous parts are separated from one another by definite surfaces; their properties differ from one another by finite amounts. Gibbs called the homogeneous portions of a thermodynamic system "phases," a name which we shall employ hereafter.

We have mentioned frequently the constituents of a system and have seen in (4) that their number is of great importance with respect to the form of the equation of state. These constituents have been considered as independent variables of the composition. That is, we have spoken of n constituents when under the same circumstances the concentrations of only $n-1$ constituents are necessary for specifying the composition of a phase. Phase theory characterizes constituents of this type as independent constituents. They are defined as the constituents whose concentrations in the several phases can be changed independently of each other. Consider a water solution of a salt. Its composition depends upon the amount of water m_{H2O} and of salt m_s, either of which can be changed independently of the other. To specify the composition it is sufficient to give the concentration of the salt, $c_s = \dfrac{m_s}{m_s + m_{H2O}}$.

As long as the composition of the solvent—in this case, water—and that of the solute (dissolved salt) do not change, the problem requires no further attention. With respect to the water, it is of no consequence whether its concentration be specified by stating the quantity of hydrogen, or of oxygen, or of the water itself, since in any case the concentration is given by a number. The same conditions hold for the salt— *e.g.*, common salt. A system composed of water is a one-component system so long as the same proportion of oxygen and hydrogen is present in all phases, which is the condition existing at ordinary temperatures. However, at higher temperatures, at which water dissociates appreciably into hydrogen and oxygen, the gas phase will generally have a different ratio of hydrogen to oxygen from that existing in steam. Such a system, even when its average composition corresponds to water, as will be the case when only water was taken initially, must be considered a two-component system.

* Note by translator: Only two of these are really independent, although any pair may be selected.

Let us consider more in detail the system hydrogen, oxygen, and water at low temperatures; this system is composed of three independent components. No reaction between hydrogen and oxygen occurs, and there is no dissociation of water. Hence, to specify the composition of any phase —for example, the gas phase—it is necessary to state the amount of each of the three independent constituents, hydrogen, oxygen, and water. On the other hand, if the system is carried to temperatures at which dissociation occurs and oxygen and hydrogen react with each other, there exists a relation between the concentrations of H_2, O_2, and H_2O of the form

$$K = \frac{c_{H_2}^2 \cdot c_{O_2}}{c_{H_2O}^2} \tag{5}$$

known as the Mass Law. When such a relation exists between the various concentrations, these are no longer independent of each other. For example, if the mass of oxygen and the mass of hydrogen are specified, the mass of water is known from (5). Because of this relation, the number of independent variables has decreased by one and we have again arrived at a system with two components.

The quantitative relationships between the pressure, the temperature, and the concentrations of the constituents in the different phases and also the various equations of state which indicate the conditions existing within the separate phases are extremely complicated for systems with a number of components—in fact, for even a two-component system. For this reason, little use is made of these relationships in discussions of heterogeneous equilibria.

The fundamental statements of thermodynamics, which are used constantly, refer to the number of possible changes in a system and the number of phases existing in it. The formal expression of the relation between these two numbers forms the content of the phase rule. This rule is generally written as

$$p + f = n + 2, \tag{6}$$

where p is the number of phases present in the system, n the number of independent constituents, and f the number of possible independent changes of state of this system. The number of possible independent changes of state of the system is usually called the "number of degrees of freedom." The system is called invariant, mono-variant, bi-variant, tri-variant, and so on, according to whether it possesses 0, 1, 2, 3, etc. degrees of freedom.

For a system of one constituent, like water, the phase rule takes the form

$$p + f = 3. \tag{7}$$

If the system consists of one phase—for instance, the gaseous—$f = 2$, that is, there are two degrees of freedom. Thus, we can actually change two variables in any way desired—for example, the pressure and the temperature—and fix the volume automatically. If, on the other hand, there are two phases, as for water vapor in equilibrium with liquid water, $p=2$ and therefore $f=1$. In this case, for every temperature there corresponds a fixed vapor pressure and hence also a definite specific volume for the vapor. There is, therefore, only one independent variable; and since the same considerations hold for the liquid water as for the vapor, the state of both phases is completely determined when this variable is fixed. Next, if $p=3$, which is the case at the melting point of ice, both liquid water and vapor being assumed present, $f=0$—that is, there are no degrees of freedom and the system is completely fixed. These three phases can exist simultaneously at only one given pressure and temperature, and hence the specific volume and the other properties of all phases are fixed at the melting point. If an attempt is made to raise the temperature by supplying heat to the system, the system opposes the change by having part of the ice melt so that the temperature remains constant. This condition holds until all the ice has melted, after which the temperature will rise for further additions of heat. However, there is now one phase less and correspondingly one additional degree of freedom. This analysis shows that for a one-component system, the phase rule is simply the formal expression of common experience.

In the same way the phase rule may be applied to systems of more than one component. Let us consider briefly the case of a ternary system where $n=3$ and the phase rule takes the form

$$p+f=5. \tag{8}$$

For a homogeneous phase—for example, a liquid alloy—there will be four degrees of freedom, as will be seen from the following. It is possible to change both the temperature and the pressure arbitrarily and, within certain limits, the two concentrations c_1 and c_2. There are therefore actually four variables which can be changed as desired. If the composition and also the pressure and temperature are fixed, then all the properties are determined, which is another way of saying that the state of the alloy is established.

For the remainder of this book, we shall consider the restricted case in which the vapor pressure of the alloy is to be neglected. The state of the alloy under atmospheric pressure is approximately the same as for a condensed system. By a "condensed system" is understood one which is under a pressure greater than the vapor pressure of the substance, so that the vapor phase does not exist at all. If the pressure is held constant, one degree of freedom is lost and (8), specifying the phase rule for a ternary system, is changed to

$$p+f=4. \tag{9}$$

Further consideration of the system will be taken up on this basis.

A homogeneous system with $p=1$ has three degrees of freedom—the temperature and the two independent concentrations—which determine the composition. Hence, for the geometric representation of such a homogeneous system three dimensions are required.

If a system consists of two phases—for example, one melt and one crystalline phase—there will be only two degrees of freedom. If the composition of the alloy is fixed, both of the independent variables will be used up and the temperature will be exactly defined. Therefore, two co-existing phases will be represented not by a state space but a state surface.

For the case when three phases are present, only one degree of freedom remains, or only one composition variable can be selected arbitrarily. When the value of this variable has been selected, the temperature and the other concentration variables are also fixed. The geometric representation of three simultaneously existing phases is a space curve. Examples which will be met frequently are the curves which correspond to doubly saturated melts (binary eutectic melts).

If there are four phases present there can be no degree of freedom at all. The system can exist at only one temperature and the compositions of all the phases are fixed.

In its usual form as given in (6), the phase rule has a formal and artificial appearance which brings to mind no physical images. For this reason, a brief and clarifying but not completely rigorous derivation will be given. The reader will note how extraordinarily simple the derivation is and how closely it is related to everyday experience.

Consider a system of n components. If it consists of only one phase, it will have an equation of state with a total of $n+2$ variables as illustrated by (4). Of these only $n+1$ will be independent, for when numbers are arbitrarily selected for $n+1$ variables, the remaining variable can have only one value. This statement is equivalent to saying that the system has $n+1$ degrees of freedom, which is exactly the result obtained by substituting 1 for p in (6). Hence, the phase rule has already been derived for the case of one homogeneous phase.

Next consider a system composed of two phases. For each of these there will be an equation of the kind represented by (4); hence the system will have two equations of state,

$$F^1(c_1^1, c_2^1, \ldots, c_{n-1}^1, PTV^1) = 0$$
$$F^2(c_1^2, c_2^2, \ldots, c_{n-1}^2, PTV^2) = 0, \tag{10}$$

where the constituents are represented by the subscripts and the phases by the superscripts. P and T will be the same throughout the system, but the values of the concentrations and the specific volume will differ in the two phases. The concentrations in the second phase are not independent of those in the first, for the concentration of each constituent, c_K^2, is determined by the state of the first phase—that is, by the concentration variables and temperature of the latter according to the equation:

$$c_K^2 = f(c_1^1, c_2^1, \ldots, c_{n-1}^1, TPV^1).$$ (11)

This equation is the general form of the law of the distribution of the constituents between the phases. An example of the dependence of the concentrations in the second phase upon those in the first phase is the case of water vapor over a solution of common salt in a mixture of water and alcohol. Since an equation similar to (11) may be obtained for each independent constituent, there will be n equations like (11).

Looking over the situation as a whole, n new variables have been added as a result of the presence of the second phase. On the other hand, $n+1$ new relations have been obtained—that is, one equation of state and n equations similar to (11). The number of independent variables has decreased by one, as has also the number of degrees of freedom. For one phase, there were $n+1$ degrees of freedom, but there are only n now.* The phase rule has been satisfied also in this case.

Upon proceeding in this way to a system with more phases, it will be found that for each new phase added there will be introduced n new variables and $n+1$ new equations. Hence, for each new phase added, one independent variable (or otherwise expressed—one degree of freedom) is lost. This statement is completely equivalent to saying that the sum of the number of phases and the number of degrees of freedom is constant, as stated mathematically in (6). Actually, the constant is $n+2$, as was obtained immediately for the homogeneous system.

If some external influence is exerted upon a system of one or more degrees of freedom—for example, the addition of heat—the temperature

---

* Note by translator: The decrease in the number of degrees of freedom in the case of two phases may be analyzed in a little greater detail. There are $n+2$ variables in the first equation of state and n more (new) ones in the second equation of state, or a total of $2n+2$ variables. The total number of equations has been shown above to be $n+2$. Treatises on algebra show that in a system of n equations in n or more variables the number of variables to which values may be arbitrarily assigned is equal to the excess of the number of variables over the number of equations. In our case the number of independent variables—that is, variables to which values may be assigned according to individual fancy—is $2n+2-(n+2)=n$. A simple algebraic system in three equations and four variables would be

$$a_1x + b_1y + c_1z + d_1t = 0,$$
$$a_2x + b_2y + c_2z + d_2t = 0,$$
$$a_3x + b_3y + c_3z + d_3t = 0.$$

The value of any one of the variables, as z, may be selected according to whim, but the system then becomes one of three variables and three equations so that the values of the remaining variables are fixed by the numerical values of the coefficients. In this case the excess of variables over equations was 1, which is the number of variables to which an arbitrary value may be given. It is also the result obtained if $n=1$ in the expression $2n+2-(n+2)$.

will usually be changed and, simultaneously, the composition and relative amounts of the phases. The conditions are different for an invariant system. Since there are no degrees of freedom, the pressure, the temperature, and also the compositions of the various phases must remain constant. Therefore, if heat be added to such a system, only the amounts of the phases can vary. Changes of this type come about through the movement of material from some phases into others, and may continue until one of them is consumed.

2. Geometric Fundamentals

It has been mentioned that the composition of a ternary system is established by two of the variables, as c_A and c_B, which specify the concentrations of the components A and B respectively. The concentration of the third component is obtained by subtracting the sum of these concentrations from 1, since the sum of all three concentrations is taken as equal to unity,

$$c_A + c_B + c_C = 1. \tag{12}$$

The composition of a ternary system may be represented on a plane in either of two ways. In the one, the perpendicular coordinate system

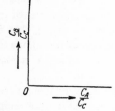

Fig. 1.
Method of plotting compositions in a ternary system with emphasis on the component C.

may be employed as shown in Fig. 1, in which the coordinates are the ratios,

$$\frac{c_A}{c_C} \text{ and } \frac{c_B}{c_C}.$$

This method of representation is useful if one of the three components predominates, as in the case of a solvent. It will be seen that the origin of the coordinate system represents the concentrations $c_A = c_B = 0$; $c_C = 1$, corresponding to the pure solvent. The pure components A and B, which correspond to the value of $c_C = 0$, are plotted at infinity; consequently their concentrations cannot appear in the diagram. This method will not be employed in the present treatise.

For ternary systems in which the three components generally have the same relative importance, it is usual to employ an equilateral triangle.

Such a triangle has the property that the sum of the lengths of the three perpendiculars from any interior point M to the three sides is constant and equal to the height h (Fig. 2). If the height h is taken as 1, and each of the perpendiculars Ma, Mb, Mc, is equal to the concentrations c_A, c_B, and c_C, each point in the interior of the triangle will correspond to a definite composition in the ternary system. We are thus provided with a very satisfactory method of representing the composition.

Obviously, the corners of the triangle correspond to the pure components, for at these points two of the perpendiculars to the sides of the triangle equal 0 and the third is equal to 1. The percentage of a particular component, as A in an alloy, is obtained by finding the corresponding perpendicular distance from the point to the opposite side. The greater the distance of the point from A, the shorter Ma will be. When the length Ma becomes 0, the alloy contains no A, and since the point lies on the side BC, it represents a binary alloy of B with C. In a similar manner the side AB represents the binary alloys of A with B, and side AC, the binary alloys of A with C.

All alloys whose compositions are represented by points on the line mn, which is parallel to BC, contain the same amount of A, since the perpendicular distance from mn to BC is constant. Similarly, all alloys which contain the same amount of B lie on a line parallel to AC, and all alloys which contain the same amount of C lie on a line parallel to AB. Alloys which lie on a line like CD that passes through the corner C, are characterized by a constant ratio of the other two components A and B, because for all points on such a line the ratio of the perpendicular distance to the sides AC and BC is the same.

Fig. 2.

Method of plotting compositions in a ternary system with all components having equal importance.

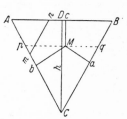

The ratio of the perpendicular distance cM (Fig. 2) to the height CD is the same as the ratio of qB ($=pA$) to the length of the side AC ($=BC$). For this reason it is immaterial in specifying the concentration whether the height CD or one of the sides is taken as unity. In the one case, the concentration of C at the point M is read cM and in the other, qB ($=pA$).

In practice it is customary to express the concentrations in per cent —that is, the sum of the three concentrations is set equal to 100. The sides of the triangle are divided into 100 parts to provide a scale for indicating the concentration of each constituent. In order to obtain the concentration in C of a point M, a line pq is drawn parallel to the opposite side AB and the distance pA (or qB) of the intersections of this line with the sides from the corners A and B is measured off. The ratio of pA to the length of a side then represents the concentration in C of an alloy corresponding in composition to the point M.

Consider a mixture of two ternary alloys of the compositions M and N (Fig. 3) and having masses m and n. The problem is to determine the composition of the mixture. The rule here is similar to that in binary systems. The final composition, P, of such a mixture always lies on the straight line joining the points M and N, and its position is determined from the masses m and n through the law of levers:

$$\frac{PN}{MP} = \frac{m}{n}.$$

Although use will occasionally be made of this law, its rather simple geometric derivation will not be discussed. In this case, as in all matters relating to the over-all composition of alloys made up of mixtures of several other alloys of partial systems, the state of the contributing alloys is a matter of no importance. For example, the points M and N may each represent homogeneous phases, or quite as readily, simply mixtures of components which have not even been melted together. Regardless of these conditions, the composition of the mixture P is the same.

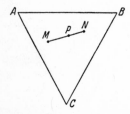

FIG. 3. Law of the straight combining line for mixtures of two structural constituents.

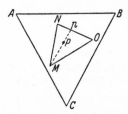

FIG. 4. Three structural constituents in a three-component system and the law of the center of gravity.

From the law of the straight combining line it follows that if an alloy, P, breaks up into two phases, M and N (Fig. 3), the three points must lie on a straight line. Such a line connecting two phases which are in equilibrium with each other is called a "conode."[*]

In the case of a mixture of three substances or partial systems M, N, and O, in the amounts m, n, and o, respectively, the composition P lies

[*] The English "tie-line" is often used for such lines but it seems simpler to adopt the German "konode," or "conode" if the term is Anglicized.

inside the triangle MNO (Fig. 4) at the center of gravity calculated by supposing the three masses m, n, and o to be attached to the points M, N, and O. The fraction of the substance M in the mixture P is equal to the ratio of the line Pp to the total line Mp. Corresponding construction holds for the other two constituents N and O. This law, which we shall not derive here, is, as may easily be seen, an extension of the method of determining concentrations in ternary systems to the case of a triangle with unequal sides. Conversely, if an alloy, P, disintegrates into the three phases M, N, and O, its composition must lie inside of the triangle MNO.

It is evident that the law of the center of gravity need not be limited to mixtures of three components—that is, to the triangle—but holds also for mixtures of a greater number of partial systems. For example, if the problem is to determine the composition of a mixture of a parts of substance A, b parts of substance B, c parts of substance C, and d parts of substance D, the rule states that it corresponds to the center of gravity of the polygon, which is constructed in the same way as the triangle previously discussed.

Fig. 5. The eutectic arrangement of a four-phase equilibrium.

Fig. 6. The peritectic arrangement of a four-phase equilibrium.

The concepts employed above may be applied to the phases present in a ternary system. For example, if four phases coexist, they may have compositions corresponding to either Fig. 5 or Fig. 6. In the first case, the composition of one phase, d, lies inside of the triangle formed by the compositions of the other three phases a, b, and c. In the second case, the composition of each phase lies outside of the triangle formed by connecting the compositions of the other three phases.

It has already been mentioned that in the case of an invariant system, like that just described, changes of state can occur only by alterations in the amounts of the phases, not by shifts in their composition. Since the total amount and the total composition must remain unchanged, the following conclusions may be drawn from the case shown in Fig. 5. An alloy of the composition of the point d may consist either of a homogeneous phase or of a mixture of three phases a, b, and c in proportions determined by the law of the center of gravity. Therefore, there must exist the possibility of a reaction:

$$d \rightleftarrows a+b+c \tag{13}$$

in which the phases a, b, and c participate in amounts corresponding to the composition of the point d. It may be perceived immediately that any other reaction in this case is out of the question, for it is impossible to specify a different group of phases which can transform into another phase or combination of phases without change of total composition. The reaction (13) is called a eutectic reaction when a melt, d, breaks up into three solid substances a, b, and c. We see that the condition for such a reaction is that the composition of the melt lie inside of the triangle formed by the three solid substances.

The situation is otherwise for the case shown in Fig. 6. Here the composition corresponding to the intersection of the two lines ac and bd can be realized in two ways: first, through a mixture of the two phases a and c, and secondly, through a mixture of the two phases b *and* d—that is,

$$e = a + c = b + d. \tag{14}$$

Naturally, the amounts of a and c and also b and d are determined by the law of levers, so that the mixture has the composition e.

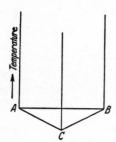

Fig. 7.

The space representation of a ternary system.

From the above, it follows that (15) is

$$a + c \rightleftharpoons b + d \tag{15}$$

a possible, and in fact the only possible reaction in this case. Such a reaction occurs when a molten material, d, reacts with one of the three solid substances, b, to produce a mixture of two other crystal types, a and c. A reaction of this kind is called a "peritectic reaction" in agreement with the nomenclature for a binary system. Thus, Fig. 6 represents the arrangement of phases corresponding to the peritectic reaction, just as Fig. 5 illustrated the case for the eutectic reaction.

It has been shown that three is the highest number of independent variables which can exist in a ternary system at constant pressure. From this fact comes the possibility of representing the states of a ternary system in a space diagram. The variables concerned are the concentrations of two of the constituents and the temperature. The diagram is usually arranged so that the concentrations are plotted on a triangle, as shown in Fig. 2, and the temperature upon an axis perpendicular to this triangle. Fig. 7 shows the resulting right-triangular prism in perspective. The edges of the prism represent the state of the three components at different temperatures. Its sides show the temperature-concentration diagrams of the binary alloys formed between each pair of the components of the ternary system. This method of representation will be used throughout this book.

Chapter II

Mechanical Mixtures Without Compounds and Without Solid Solutions

1. Process of Crystallization

Let us consider a ternary system in which the corresponding binary systems are simple mechanical mixtures of the components. They possess eutectics, but form neither solid solutions nor compounds. Furthermore, neither solid solutions nor compounds occur within the ternary system.

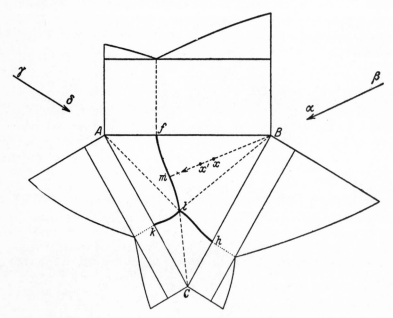

Fig. 8. The triangle of concentrations of a mechanical mixture with eutectic.

In Fig. 8 is shown the concentration triangle of such a system with the binary diagrams of the constituents of which it is composed laid out along its sides. Representation of this kind is often employed instead of a perspective arrangement. In Fig. 9 the space figure of the same

14

system may be seen in perspective. Corresponding points in the two figures are indicated by the same letters, small in one diagram and capital in the other.

Since the three metals are completely soluble in the liquid state, the system will consist of a homogeneous melt at elevated temperatures. Since only one phase is present, the system will have three degrees of freedom—that is, both the temperature and composition of the liquid alloy may be varied at will within the limits of the state space occupied by the melt.

Consider an alloy of the composition x (Fig. 8). As it cools from the temperature of the point X (Fig. 9), its representative point drops through a series of positions down the vertical line XJ to the temperature of the point J, at which freezing begins. According to hypothesis, only pure components can crystallize out; hence the process of crystallization must begin by precipitation of one of the components. Since the precipitated component comes out as solid, its solidification temperature must be higher than the melting point of the alloy. In the case illustrated in Figs. 8 and 9 the component B is the first to crystallize out of the liquid alloy of composition x.

As the crystals of B precipitate out, the amount of B in the melt must diminish. In the example shown, the alloy x has broken up into the component B and the remaining melt x'. From the law of the straight combining line (Fig. 3), the straight line connecting x' and B (Fig. 8) must pass through the point x which gives the composition of the whole alloy. This fact provides a very simple rule for the displacement of the composition of the melt during the crystallization of one of the components. The composition of the remaining melt moves along the projection of the straight line connecting the precipitated component and the composition of the entire alloy in the direction away from the point (the corner B) representing the composition of the precipitated substance.

There are now two phases which are in equilibrium with each other: the melt saturated in B and the crystalline B. According to (9), there are now only two degrees of freedom. The sequence of state points representing the melt therefore can no longer correspond to a space region like that for the homogeneous melt before freezing began, but must form a surface. This surface, which in general is curved, is called the surface of primary crystallization in analogy with the curve of primary crystallization for binary alloys. During the primary crystallization of B, the state point of the melt follows a path lying on this surface. With continued precipitation of B, the melt contains diminishing percentages of this component and simultaneously its freezing temperature becomes lower. Hence, the surface of primary precipitation of crystalline B must descend as it reaches from the B corner out into the body of the prism, something in the manner suggested by the surface $FGHL$ (Fig. 9).

On account of the loss of B during the primary precipitation process, the melt becomes relatively richer in A and C. Thus, a point must eventually be reached where it is saturated not only in B but also in one of the other constituents—for example, in A—and in this case the simultaneous crystallization of both A and B will occur. This condition is reached in point m of the diagram (Fig. 8). The system now consists of three phases, and hence can possess only one degree of freedom. Therefore, for each temperature the composition of the melt is completely specified, and *vice versa*. The sequence of points representing the doubly saturated melt will therefore no longer constitute a surface but only a space curve fl. Al-

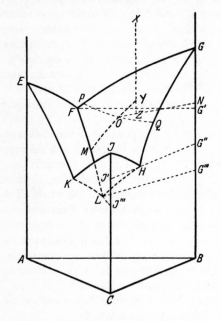

Fig. 9.

The space diagram of a mechanical mixture shown in perspective.

though in a binary system the simultaneous precipitation of two kinds of crystals at a eutectic point corresponds to an invariant equilibrium, a ternary system under such conditions still has one degree of freedom. Hence, in this case the temperature continues to sink during the process of crystallization while the composition of the melt moves along the curve fl.

The simultaneous precipitation in a ternary system of two types of crystals from a melt is designated as a binary eutectic crystallization. During this type of solidification, structures are developed which are similar to those produced in a binary system; but on account of the slower process of crystallization they are coarser and often less typical of eutectics.

The curve *FML* (Fig. 9) represents the sequence of compositions of the liquid phase saturated in A and B during the binary eutectic crystallization of these components. It begins at the eutectic point of the binary system AB and drops away into the interior of the ternary system to lower temperatures.

During the binary eutectic crystallization the remaining melt becomes richer in C. As soon as it reaches the saturation point, the simultaneous precipitation of the three components sets in. The system is then composed of four phases: melt and the three crystalline substances A, B, and C. In agreement with (9), there no longer exists any degree of freedom at all, and crystallization must henceforth proceed at constant temperature and with unchanged composition of the molten material until all of the latter is consumed—that is, until the freezing process is finished. The simultaneous crystallization of three substances is called "ternary eutectic crystallization" and corresponds to the point l (Fig. 8) or L (Fig. 9), which is said to be the ternary eutectic point.

All melts having compositions in the field $fBhl$ (Fig. 8) will precipitate component B when they begin to freeze. Similarly, melts of the field $Aflk$ will throw out component A upon reaching the surface of primary crystallization, while those of $klhC$ yield component C. All alloys having their representative points in the subtriangle AlB will first experience a primary crystallization of either A or B, at the end of which the binary eutectic crystallization of both elements together will begin. During the latter stage, the composition of the doubly saturated melt follows along the line fl. In a similar manner, the binary eutectic crystallization of A and C occurs in the subtriangle AlC, and during the process the composition of the molten portion follows a sequence of points on the curve kl. In region ClB the binary eutectic crystallization of C and B proceeds, while simultaneously the melt follows along the curve hl. Without further discussion it is obvious that, for all melts, the solidifying process eventually reaches a ternary eutectic crystallization, in which the composition of the melt and the temperature of the system correspond to the ternary eutectic point l (Fig. 8).

2. State Spaces

In a binary diagram such as the one shown in Fig. 10 two kinds of state regions may be distinguished: the homogeneous, illustrated by melt s, and the solid solutions α and β; and the heterogeneous, represented by areas $s+\alpha$, $s+\beta$, and $\alpha+\beta$—that is, regions containing two phases. The significance of the two types is quite different. Consider an alloy of the composition x. This alloy may be represented by the point m in the state region of the homogeneous melt s. The location of m then gives the temperature and composition of the phase at that temperature—that is, it specifies the state of the alloy. However, if a point lies inside of a heterogeneous field, as at n or o, it does not correspond to any actual state. For example, an alloy of composition x at the temperature of point n is composed of two phases whose compositions are given by the intersection of a horizontal line through n with the sloping lines on either side of this point. Thus the heterogeneous state regions in a binary system actually indicate gaps—that is, concentration and temperature regions inside of which there is no actual state.

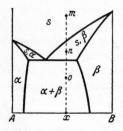

Fig. 10.

Illustration of a binary constitutional diagram.

A similar situation exists with respect to the state spaces in ternary systems, and in these systems also it is necessary to distinguish between the homogeneous and heterogeneous types. The significance of the former kind, called a "one-phase space," is obvious. The heterogeneous two- and three-phase spaces correspond to space gaps in the diagram, within which no homogeneous phase can exist. An alloy, the state point of which lies in such a space, breaks up into two or three phases with compositions lying on the surfaces which bound the space. The rule by which these compositions may be found will next be set up.

Application of these general remarks to the previously discussed case of the freezing of a ternary mechanical mixture yields the following analysis. After the process of crystallization of an alloy has begun, it proceeds throughout a definite temperature interval—that is, in this interval the alloy continues to break up into two phases: solid and melt. There is, therefore, a space of primary crystallization which is bounded above by the surface of the beginning of crystallization and below by the surface at which the binary eutectic crystallization begins. This lower surface should be pictured as the assemblage of points, each of which is defined by the coordinates giving the composition of an alloy and the temperature at which this alloy becomes saturated in two components, and therefore begins the stage of binary eutectic solidification. Evidently, the surface so generated also forms the upper limit of the space of binary eutectic crystallization. Since the binary eutectic crystallization always ends at the ternary eutectic point, the spaces of binary eutectic crystallization are bounded below by the horizontal plane passing through this point.

Let us next consider the space of primary crystallization of B (Fig. 9), and assume that after the alloy X reached the point Y upon the surface of primary crystallization, further cooling brought it to the point Z. It now exists in the space of primary crystallization of B, and the problem remaining is to find in what manner the alloy indicated by the state point Z divides into the actually existing melt and crystalline B. The rule is very simple. Since the average composition of an alloy consisting of two phases lies on the line connecting the compositions of these phases, it is necessary only to draw a horizontal line through the point Z and the edge GB of the prism of state (at point N, Fig. 9) and extend it to its point of

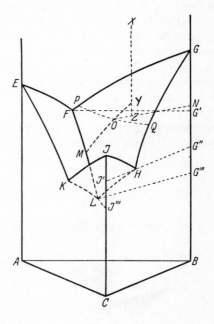

Fig. 9.

The space diagram of a mechanical mixture shown in perspective.

intersection with the surface of primary crystallization (O, Fig. 9). O specifies the composition of the melt with which B is in equilibrium at the temperature under consideration. The line OZN is evidently a conode, for it connects phases that are at the same temperature and in equilibrium.

The significance of a space of primary crystallization requires no further discussion, but it is desirable to consider more in detail the boundaries of such a space. For example, the space of primary crystallization of B is bounded above by the surface of primary crystallization $GHLFG$ (Fig. 9), and at the sides by the perpendicular planes corresponding to the areas of the binary systems A-B and B-C, in which the primary crystallization of B occurs—that is, the plane sections $GFG'G$ and $GHG''G$. In describing the lower boundary of this space it will be necessary to refer again to the primary crystallization of the alloy x according to Fig. 8. The lower limit of the space of primary crystallization of B will be at-

tained for this alloy when the binary eutectic crystallization begins—that
is, when the composition of the melt reaches the point m, which marks the
intersection of the path xx' of crystallization with the line fl of doubly
saturated melt. It is at once evident that for all alloys whose compositions lie on the line Bm, the path of crystallization will meet the curve fl
at the same point, m. Consequently, all these alloys will complete the
stage of primary crystallization at the same temperature—that of the
point m. Since the same analysis holds for the points of other lines extending from B to points on the space curve fl, the lower boundary of the
space of primary crystallization of B (separating this space from the
region of the simultaneous binary eutectic crystallization of A and B) is
generated by the motion of a horizontal line, one end of which follows the
curve fl while the other glides down the vertical axis B from higher to
lower temperatures. Since, as has been explained above, the curve fl,
or the corresponding line FL (Fig. 9), descends from F to L, there is
formed an irregular left-handed screw surface having the axis GB (Fig. 9)
and extending from FG' to LG'''. Exactly the same procedure can be
applied to the part of the space of the primary crystallization of B which

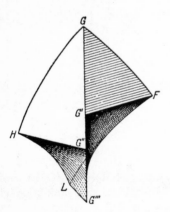

FIG. 11.

View of the space of primary
crystallization of B as seen obliquely from above and in the direction $\alpha\beta$ (Fig. 8).

is related to the binary eutectic crystallization of B and C. In this case
there is obtained a surface formed by the movement of a horizontal line
one end of which passes along the curve HL while the other glides down
the vertical axis GB (Fig. 9). At the temperature of the ternary eutectic
point these two screw surfaces meet in the line LG''', forming a rib.

The complete space of primary crystallization of B is illustrated in Fig.
11, as it appears when viewed in the direction of the arrow $\alpha\beta$ shown in
Fig. 8. The alphabetical characters correspond to those of Fig. 9. The
upper boundary surface of the state space $GFLHG$ is turned away from
the observer. The perpendicular planes $GHG''G$ and $GFG'G$ coincide
with the sides of the prism of state and are identical with the associated

binary systems. The two screw surfaces which mark the lower boundary are $G'FLG'''G'$ and $G''HLG'''G''$. The first separates the space of primary crystallization of B from that of the binary crystallization of A and B and includes alloys lying in the partial region $BflB$ (Fig. 8). The second marks it off from the region of binary eutectic crystallization of C and B and corresponds to alloys in the partial region $BlhB$ (Fig. 8). The first screw surface is left-handed; the second, right-handed. Their horizontal line of intersection LG'''' (Fig. 11) corresponds to lB in Fig. 8.

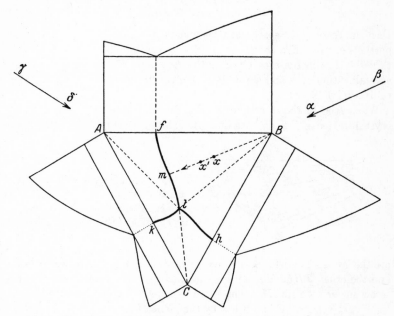

Fɪɢ. 8. The triangle of concentrations of a mechanical mixture with eutectic.

Similar space states of primary crystallization exist for the other two components. The projection of their upper limiting surfaces, which are the surfaces of the beginning of crystallization, are the curved polygons $AflkA$ and $CklhC$ in Fig. 8.

The following observations may be made concerning the form of the three spaces of primary crystallization. The upper surfaces of the spaces intersect along the lines FL, KL, and HL. Below, these spaces diverge and leave room for other regions (of binary eutectic crystallization) between the screw surfaces and the sides of the prism. Each state space is named for the phase which separates out in it; hence in the case considered, the three regions of primary crystallization are called $A+$ melt, $B+$ melt, and $C+$ melt.

The spaces of binary eutectic crystallization adjoin the under side of the spaces of primary crystallization. They exist because for each ternary alloy there is a definite temperature interval in which binary eutectic crystallization occurs. The boundaries of these spaces are easy to deduce after the discussion of the spaces of primary crystallization. It is at once clear that there must be three regions of binary eutectic crystallization which possess, respectively, the constituents:

$$A+B+\text{melt}=A+B+s,$$
$$B+C+\text{melt}=B+C+s,$$
$$C+A+\text{melt}=C+A+s.$$

Each of these state spaces can be imagined with some accuracy from portions of two different regions of primary crystallization. According as the alloy lies in the area $ChlC$ or the region $BhlB$, the binary eutectic crystallization of B and C sets in at the conclusion of the primary crystallization of B or C.

When seen in the direction $\gamma\delta$ (Fig. 8), the space of binary eutectic crystallization of B and C has the form exhibited in Fig. 12. In the front

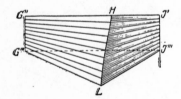

Fig. 12.

View of the space of binary eutectic crystallization of B and C as seen obliquely from above in the direction $\gamma\delta$ (Fig. 8).

are the two screw surfaces: the one, $G''HLG'''G''$, which is attached to B, and the other, $J'HLJ'''J'$, which is attached to C and forms with the first screw surface the rib HL. The space is bounded behind by the plane of the binary system BC and below by the plane of ternary eutectic crystallization. In Fig. 12 the part of the space diagram between the observer and the portion under consideration has been removed. The lettering is the same as in Fig. 9.

All intersections of horizontal, isothermal planes with the binary crystallization space are straight-sided triangles, as would be anticipated from the presence of screw surfaces. The boundaries of this space have therefore the form of a three-edged tube, of which the back wall is formed by the side of the prism, and the other two walls are the screw surfaces generated by the motion of two straight lines whose outer ends are connected to the corners of the prism representing the pure components, and whose inner ends glide down the curve HL (Fig. 9). This tube-like space is constricted in its uppermost section to the straight line $G''J'$, which lies in the binary system BC. The conditions are very similar for the binary eutectic crystallization of A and B and A and C.

On the basis of the above discussion, it is possible to specify the composition and amount of the phases into which an alloy disintegrates if its composition lies in the interior of a three-phase space. The composition of the various phases is given by the corners of the isothermal triangle (Fig. 12), and their amount by the center of gravity relation.

Upon completing the binary eutectic crystallization the alloy encounters the ternary eutectic crystallization. The latter does not have a state space in our representation but only an isothermal plane because the process takes place at constant temperature.

With the completion of the ternary eutectic crystallization, the process of solidification is finished. Since any alloy consists of three kinds of crystals—*A*, *B*, and *C*—we are evidently dealing again with a three-phase space. The difference between this three-phase space and those previously considered is that the composition of all three phases is now independent of the temperature, since the crystals are composed of pure components. The three-cornered tube stands vertically and coincides with the prism of state.

The prism of state of a ternary mixture with a eutectic is divided into eight spaces: the homogeneous space of the melt, the three spaces of primary crystallization, the three three-cornered spaces of binary eutectic crystallization, and the region of the completely solid alloy.

When an alloy cools, the state point representing it, in general, passes through four regions: first, the region of the melt; then the spaces of primary and binary eutectic crystallization; and finally, the solid state. In homogeneous spaces each point corresponds to a thermodynamically possible state, whereas inside of the heterogeneous spaces each point corresponds to an alloy which has the specified composition but has broken up into two or three phases. In a two-phase system the two phases lie upon a conode which passes through the point representing the total composition of the alloy. In the three-phase space the phases lie at the corners of a triangle which includes the total composition.

3. STATE SURFACES

The state surfaces in a ternary system are the boundaries separating the different state spaces. The significance of such surfaces differs, depending upon the spaces of which they form the boundary. A surface may divide a homogeneous phase of molten material or a solid solution from a two-phase space; or it may separate a two-phase space, such as a region of primary crystallization, from a three-phase space such as a region of binary eutectic crystallization. In the first case, the meaning is clear; the surface gives the temperature and the composition of melt or of solid solution saturated in a second phase. In the case of the beginning of crystallization of a mechanical mixture, the surface is called a "surface of primary crystallization," and specifies the composition of the melt with which the precipitated crystalline substance is in equilibrium at the given temperature. The situation is different for the boundary surface between the spaces of primary and binary eutectic crystallization. A point inside of either heterogeneous system does not correspond to any possible state of the system and therefore neither can a point on the boundary between such regions. The boundary surface between two such spaces is composed of a series of conodes, and the only information a conode can give is to specify for the given temperature the compositions and amounts of the two phases composing an alloy which has a composition represented by a point thereon. The point itself corresponds to no possible state of the system. In general, it may be said concerning such surfaces that the points lying on them correspond to no possible state of the system, but only give information concerning the two phases out of which the system is built up, in the same manner as a point in one of the adjoining spaces. The boundary surface may be assumed to have associated with it the number of phases present in the adjoining space containing the fewer—in this instance, two; for the amount of the third phase in the three-phase space is zero at the boundary. The boundary comes into existence because over this boundary surface the alloys of the two-phase space have become saturated in the third phase.

The plane of ternary eutectic crystallization presents an exceptional case, since it corresponds to an equilibrium of four phases and is the boundary between spaces having three phases. This situation occurs because the plane actually is a degenerated state space which can exist at only one temperature.

Since the state surfaces yield no information besides that furnished by the state spaces, they will not be considered in later chapters.

4. ISOTHERMAL SECTIONS

In analyzing ternary systems the need often arises for gaining a comprehensive view of all the phases which exist in equilibrium at some definite temperature. For this purpose an isothermal section through the space diagram is of considerable aid.

To examine our present system let us consider again Figs. 8 and 9 and observe the nature of the isothermal sections which develop as the temperature decreases. At high temperatures before the beginning of solidification the whole concentration triangle is composed of a homogeneous melt, and no phase boundaries exist. Below the temperature at which the primary crystallization of B sets in but still above the melting point of both the other components, the section will show, besides the region of the melt, the heterogeneous region of the primary crystallization of B.

If the state prism (Fig. 9) is cut at the temperature of point Z by a horizontal plane (isothermal section), the schematic diagram shown in

Fig. 13 is obtained. The curve *pq* is the intersection of the horizontal plane with the surface of primary crystallization *FGHLF* of *B* in Fig. 9. The curve *tr* is the corresponding intersection with the surface of primary crystallization of *A*. The solidification of *C* has not yet set in. The

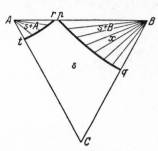

Fig. 13.

Isothermal section at the temperature of the point *O* (Fig. 9).

region *trpqCt* indicates the composition of the alloys which, at the temperature under consideration, are still liquid. The areas *rAt* and *pBq* are sections through spaces of primary crystallization. Consider an alloy represented by a point lying in one of these areas—for example, *x* in *pBq*.

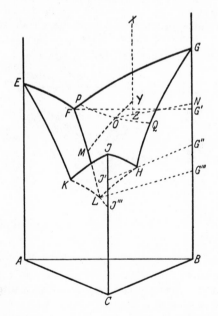

Fig. 9.

The space diagram of a mechanical mixture shown in perspective.

The composition of the melt remaining after the solid component, *B*, has separated to the extent prescribed by the given temperature is determined by the point *o* at which a straight line extending from *B* through *x* strikes the boundary *pq*. In Fig. 13, and in later illustrations of isothermal sections in which two phase areas of primary crystallization are being considered, a system of fine lines representing conodes is employed to show the composition of the coexisting phases.

It is instructive to compare the diagram of Fig. 8 with that of Fig. 13. The first represents the projection of the prism (Fig. 9) on its basal plane;

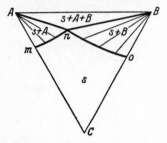

Fig. 14. Isothermal section after the beginning of the binary eutectic crystallization of *A* and *B*.

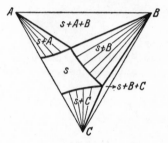

Fig. 15. Isothermal section after the beginning of the second binary eutectic crystallization.

the second shows a section through the prism. It must be obvious therefore that the two diagrams exhibit quite different data and should not be confused with each other. The curves *fl*, *lh*, and so on, which are shown in Fig. 8, do not lie at a fixed temperature and no information can be obtained from them regarding the coexisting state points. On the other

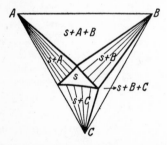

Fig. 16. Isothermal section at the temperature of the eutectic point in the system *AC*.

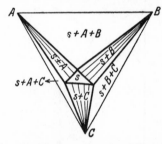

Fig. 17. Isothermal section below the binary eutectic point in the system *AC*.

hand, it is the principal purpose of an isothermal section like that in Fig. 13 to present a view of the coexisting phases at some selected temperature.

If the temperature drops still further so that the binary eutectic crystallization of *A* and *B* occurs, the situation shown in Fig. 14 will be obtained. In this diagram the alloys of the partial region *ABn* have already passed from the region of primary crystallization into the space of the binary eutectic crystallization of *A* and *B*, with consequent creation of the triangle *ABn*. The alloys of the partial region *nBo* are composed of crystalline *B* and residual melt having concentrations corresponding to points on the boundary curve *no*. Alloys in the field *mnA* disintegrate into crystalline *A* and melts with compositions along the line *mn*. The area *mnoC* is still homogeneous liquid.

A section below the melting point of *C* and the binary eutectic point *H*, but still above *K* (Fig. 9) is shown in Fig. 15. Besides the regions of primary crystallization there now exist two areas of binary eutectic crystallization. The section obtained at the temperature of the binary eutectic in the system *AC* is shown in Fig. 16. At a still lower temperature but above the ternary eutectic point, the diagram shown in Fig. 17 results. These two figures are understandable without additional discussion. At the temperature of the ternary eutectic, the region of the melt *s* shrinks to a point, the areas of primary crystallization exist only as the ribs *LG'''*, etc. (Fig. 12), and the fields of binary eutectic crystallization come into contact with each other. Below this temperature, the entire system consists of a heterogeneous mixture of the three components *A*, *B*, and *C*.

5. SECTIONS PERPENDICULAR TO THE PLANE OF CONCENTRATION

Vertical sections through the space diagram—that is, sections which are perpendicular to the basal plane of the state prims—have a different significance from those described above. They permit the course of a particular alloy to be followed during the freezing process, and for this reason are valuable in studying the changes of state of the various alloy compositions.

In examining a complete ternary system, it is usual to select the concentrations to be investigated according to a definite system. Generally the selection will be made so that the compositions lie on straight lines in the concentration triangle. Upon these lines the perpendicular sections are erected from the results obtained by studying the state of the alloys at different temperatures. As a rule, two kinds of sections are chosen. The one starts from a corner—for example, from pure component *A* (Fig. 18, section *Aq*)—and is characterized by the facts that the ratio of the amounts of the two components *B* and *C* is the same for all points and that the amount of *A* decreases in going toward the opposite side *BC*. The other type of section lies parallel to a side of the triangle, as *mn* in Fig. 21. For such a section the amount of the component located in the opposite corner—*C* in this case—is constant, while that of the other two constituents changes from zero to a maximum. In general, the kind of sections selected depends upon the nature of the system being investigated.

Let us derive some typical sections for the case under discussion. Fig. 18 shows again the concentration triangle; *fl*, *hl*, and *kl* are the curves of the doubly saturated melt and *l* is the ternary eutectic point. We shall select the section *mB* which passes through the corner *B*. As is obvious from Fig. 9, the intersection of the plane of this section with the surface of the beginning of crystallization has the form of the curve acb (Fig. 19), with a cusp at c produced by the intersection of mB with the curve of binary eutectic crystallization fl (Fig. 18). From all alloys of the portion cB (Fig. 18) crystalline B is first precipitated. This process is complete when the composition of the residual molten substance reaches the point c (Fig. 18), and the next development is the binary eutectic crystallization of A and B simultaneously. For all the alloys, the field of primary precipitation of B is limited below by the horizontal line cd (Fig. 19). This line is one of the isothermal conodes, previously discussed, which by their motion generate the screw-type upper surface of the space of binary eutectic crystallization. The space of binary eutectic crystallization of A and B together is seen below the isothermal line cd.

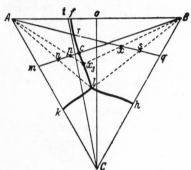

FIG. 18. Position of the vertical section diagrams mB and Aq.

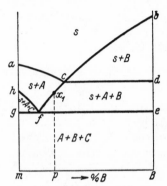

FIG. 19. Section mB (Fig. 18).

For the alloys of the portion mc (Fig. 18), the primary crystallization of A takes place first. The point representing the composition of the melt moves along the conode extending out from A and encounters, for the alloys lying between n and c, the curve fl somewhere in the interval cl. Hence, for these alloys also, the primary crystallization of A is followed by the binary eutectic crystallization of A and B. The more nearly the composition of the alloy approaches that of point n, the lower will be the temperature at which the simultaneous precipitation of both components begins. In Fig. 19 the curve cf represents the beginning of this binary eutectic crystallization. For the alloy n (Fig. 18) the ternary eutectic crystallization takes place immediately at the conclusion of the primary crystallization. Alloys in the interval mn undergo, at the conclusion of the crystallization of A, a binary eutectic crystallization of a different type—namely, that of A and C. Curve hf in Fig. 19 represents this process in the binary section mB. At the conclusion of these binary eutectic crystallizations, the solidification of the ternary eutectic mixture takes place at the temperature of the horizontal line *ge*.

Although the diagram of a binary system permits the composition of all the phases existing in equilibrium to be read off directly, the same statement does not hold in the case of a plane section of a ternary system. To be sure, the curve *acb* shows, for the melts lying in the plane of the cut, the composition at the time crystallization begins, but similar conclusions cannot be drawn from the other curves. For example, the points on the curves *hf* and *fc* merely represent intersections of conodes with the plane of the cut. In general, the phases which are in equilibrium with each other do not lie in the plane of the cut—a fact which will be appreciated after a brief study of the line *hf* (Fig. 19), which is related to the equilibrium between crystalline *A* and the melts along the line *kl* of Fig.

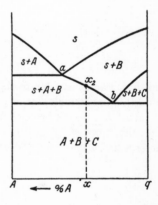

Fig. 20.

Section *Aq* (Fig. 18).

18.* In general it is impossible to reach any conclusions concerning composition by means of plane-section diagrams. Consider, for example, the ternary eutectic point which, in the cut of Fig. 19, corresponds to alloy *n* on the line *mB* (Fig. 18). Concerning its position in the ternary diagram, the only thing which can be determined from the plane section is that it lies somewhere on the projection of the line *An*. It is quite possible to locate the ternary eutectic point, however, by using a second section diagram—for example, *Aq*—in which it may be shown that the ternary eutectic point lies on the projection of the line *Bs*. The intersection of the lines *Bs* and *An* gives the desired information. The cut *Aq*, represented in Fig. 20, is very similar to the cut *mB*.

A similar procedure may be employed to determine the position of a curve of binary eutectic crystallization. Consider, in Fig. 18, the interval

---

* Note by translator: The points *h* and *f* correspond to *k* and *l*, respectively, and in general there is a one-to-one correspondence between the points of these two lines. By tracing, mentally, the solidification process of alloys lying on the portion *mn* of *mB*, the development of *hf* can be readily imagined.

rs of *Aq* representing alloys for which the primary crystallization of *B* is followed by the binary crystallization of *A* and *B*, as indicated by the curve of doubly saturated melt *rl* (Fig. 18). The points of the curve *ab* (Fig. 20) are the intersection points of the conodes combining *B* and the corresponding points of curve *rl* with the vertical plane *Aq*. From the position of the point x_2, corresponding to the alloy *x* (Fig. 18), it can be

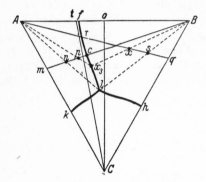

Fig. 18.

Position of the vertical section diagrams *mB* and *Aq*.

deduced in a manner similar to that employed for the ternary eutectic point that the corresponding point on the curve *rl* lying at the same temperature must fall on the projection of the line *Bx*. The next step is to locate on the curve *cf* (Fig. 19), which also corresponds to the binary eutectic crystallization along the curve *fl*, a point x_1 lying at the same

Fig. 19.

Section *mB* (Fig. 18).

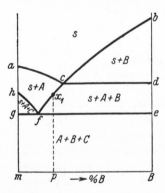

temperature as x_2, and then to find its position *p* in the binary section of Fig. 19 and on the concentration plane of Fig. 18. The curve of melt simultaneously saturated in *A* and *B* will have, at the temperature of the points x_1 and x_2, the concentration point which is the intersection of the two lines *Ap* and *Bx* (that is, the position x_3). This method is applicable to the determination of the position of the interval *cl* of the line *fl*. The necessary condition for carrying out the above construction is the definite establishment of the fact that the two curves considered, ab and cf, are actually connected with the same binary eutectic crystallization.

An assumption which underlies the establishment of a curve of doubly saturated melt is that the same curve of binary eutectic crystallization (in the present case, fl) is reached through both of the cuts under consideration. To determine the full length of a curve such as fl, it is recommended to place the cuts so that at the side AB (Fig. 18) they come as close to f as is possible without cutting the line fl—for example, in positions illustrated by Ct and Co. The cut Ct is very similar to that of Bm in Fig. 19, particularly in having a curve which corresponds to hf. This curve is related to the line fl in the same way that hf is to kl. It lies below the field of primary crystallization of A in the same way as does hf in the section Bm (Fig. 18). Through an extension of the series of conodes which pass through A and B, respectively, in the manner similar to that portrayed above, the position of the curve fl may be constructed from the intersection points of the projections of the conodes.

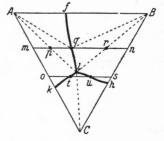

Fig. 21.

Position of the vertical sections mn and os.

Let us now consider the cuts which are taken parallel to a side of the concentration triangle. We may select section mn (Fig. 21). The curve aqc (Fig. 22) of the beginning of crystallization possesses a kink at q produced by crossing the curve of binary eutectic crystallization fl. In the interval mp the primary crystallization of A is followed by the binary eutectic crystallization of A and C together, it being understood that p lies at the intersection of the line mn with the conode extending from A to l. In the interval pq, which extends from p to the point q where mn crosses the binary eutectic curve fl, there occurs first the crystallization of A and then the simultaneous crystallization of A and B. These facts will appear in the diagram of the cut mn (Fig. 22) which shows the lines mp and pq marking the beginning of the binary eutectic solidification. The solidification process in the interval qn proceeds in a manner similar to that for mq; hence, Fig. 22 requires no elaboration. Solidification ends at the ternary eutectic point existing at the temperature of the line l_1l_2.

The cut mn (Fig. 22) offers the possibility of determining the ternary

eutectic point without the assistance of another vertical section. The
desired point lies at the intersection of the extensions of the two lines Ap
and Br (Fig. 21); hence, it is necessary only to determine in the section of
Figure 22 the positions of p and r in order to draw these lines and so
establish the position of the ternary eutectic point l. This cut also offers
the possibility of determining the position of the part ql of the curve of the
melt saturated in both A and B, for both pq and qr (Fig. 22) correspond
to the same binary eutectic crystallization along ql. It is therefore necessary only to pick off two points at the same temperature on pq and qr and
to extend through these, the corresponding conodes from A and B to their
place of intersection. This intersection lies on the curve ql. Thus, the
branches pq and qr (Fig. 22) yield the same information as can be obtained from the two corresponding curve branches fc and ab in the sections
mB and Aq, respectively (Figs. 19 and 20).

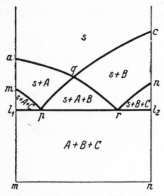

Fig. 22. Section mn (Fig. 21).

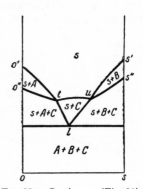

Fig. 22a. Section os (Fig. 21).

For comparison, the section os perpendicular to the plane of concentration will be developed, since it shows a typical deviation in form from
the cut mn (Fig. 22a). In the part ot (Fig. 21) the primary crystallization of A occurs; in the part tu the first solidification is that of the component C; while in part us, B crystallizes out first. Thus, the curve of
primary crystallization $o'tus'$ (Fig. 22a) consists of three branches. At
the conclusion of the primary crystallization of A there occurs in the part
ot the crystallization of the binary eutectic $A+C$, and the farther the
alloy is away from the point o of the binary side AC (curve $o''t$, Fig. 22)
the lower will be the temperature at which this begins. This situation
comes about because the path of crystallization encounters the curve of
binary eutectic crystallization kl at a correspondingly lower temperature,
the farther the alloy is distant from o. Upon passing the point t, there
takes place at the conclusion of the primary crystallization of C and up to

the intersection with the line Cl (Fig. 21), the precipitation of the same binary eutectic. For the alloy lying on the line Cl, the ternary eutectic crystallization at the point l follows directly after the conclusion of the primary crystallization of C. At the right of this intersection the alloys repeat essentially the same fundamental performance which has been pictured for those lying on the left, only that the component B is substituted for A.

Some consideration will show that the curve tl (Fig. 22a) cannot be a continuation of $o''t$, but that there must be at t a cusp in the boundary curve of the field $s+A+C$ as a consequence of the difference between the adjoining phase fields to the left and right of t, these being in the one case $s+A$ and in the other, $s+C$. The reason for these statements may be found by studying the space of binary eutectic crystallization shown in Fig. 12. In the case being considered this space will be intersected by the vertical section in the rib HL. The slope of the curve made by the intersection of the vertical plane with the bounding surface $HJ'J'''L$ on one side of the rib HL must be different from that produced by intersection with the surface $HG''G'''L$ on the other side. A similar intersection of a field of binary eutectic crystallization will be encountered in Chapter IV (Fig. 44).

Fig. 12.

View of the space of binary eutectic crystallization of B and C as seen obliquely from above in the direction $\gamma\delta$ (Fig. 8).

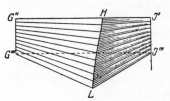

In the discussion of the crystallization of ternary systems the deductive method has hitherto been employed. We have assumed the constitution, constructed the ternary space diagram on the basis of the assumed characteristics, and finally built up the corresponding binary sections. In any actual experimental case the reverse process would be followed. The ternary space diagram must really be derived from the plane-section diagrams determined experimentally—for example, by thermal analysis. The looseness of the relationship between the vertical sections and the ternary diagram has been shown. It is for this reason that the construction of the latter on the basis of the former is difficult and uncertain. In all complex cases it is necessary to increase the number of the alloys investigated to a point where the horizontal section diagrams, as shown in Figs. 13 to 17, may be established with certainty. As has been mentioned, these diagrams permit the immediate deduction of many conclusions concerning the form of the complex state diagram.

On the other hand, it is possible in many cases to obtain some knowledge of the ternary diagram from the form of the binary diagrams. Since ternary compounds involving all three components are seldom found, it may be assumed with considerable probability that if the binary systems consist only of mechanical mixtures without solubility gaps in the liquid state, the ternary diagram will be of the simplest type just discussed. The general outlines of the system may then be traced out on the concentration triangle on the basis of the position of the eutectic points in the binary systems and further investigation limited primarily to the exact determination of the position of the eutectic curves and the ternary eutectic point, disregarding the surfaces of primary crystallization of which the determination presents no difficulty but is usually of no great interest.

Supplement to Chapter II

A General Law Concerning Contiguous State Spaces

The detailed view over the space figure of a ternary mechanical mixture and its associated horizontal and vertical sections which has been obtained in the previous discussion presents the opportunity for demonstrating a general conformity to law which often aids materially in understanding ternary systems and permits errors to be discovered readily.

We have observed that the homogeneous single-phase space of the melt is bounded by the two-phase spaces of primary crystallization, and that the latter in turn are contiguous to the three-phase spaces of binary eutectic crystallization. Further, the single-phase space has contact with the three-phase spaces only along various lines and not over surfaces. A state space can ordinarily be bounded by another state space only if the number of phases in the second space is one less or one greater than that in the first space considered. This condition is not accidental, but is based on a law of which the validity is unrestricted, except that the phase rule sets a limit to the maximum number of phases. A three-phase space cannot be bounded by a four-phase space because the latter equilibrium does not exist in the temperature-concentration prism. A four-phase structure cannot exist except at a fixed temperature and is therefore restricted to a horizontal plane. Later, we shall go somewhat further into this case although, in general, there is no exception to the rule. It is impossible for a homogeneous single-phase space to be bounded by another single-phase space or by a three-phase space. Furthermore, a two-phase space can be bounded by a one or a three-phase space but not by another two-phase space. It is easy to perceive that this law is thermodynamically necessary.

Let us consider in detail some state space—for example, a two-phase space. The border of this region will be reached whenever the combination of phases existing in it ceases to be stable. This situation may occur in only two ways. First, a point of concentration or temperature may be reached at which another phase can be precipitated out—for example, a melt may become saturated in a second crystalline substance. The alloy then enters a three-phase region, a type of phase space which is permissible according to the phase rule and must therefore exist, for all the consequences of the phase rule rest upon the fact that the available number of degrees of freedom (which is variable and depends upon the conditions) must actually be used. A two-phase space cannot border a four-phase space, as is obvious from the following remarks. Were this true, then the melt mentioned above could become saturated simultaneously with two other phases in addition to the one with which it was in equilibrium in the two-phase space. Such a condition is a special case and is possible only for certain definite concentrations; hence it can correspond to points or curves only. In general, saturation will be attained for only one of the phases. Secondly, the alloy may enter a one-phase space. That a two-phase space may border a single-phase space is self-evident from this discussion, for it is necessary only to reverse the order of reasoning and to inquire what region a one-phase space can border. It is at once obvious that the answer must be a two-phase space.

It may also be demonstrated that the number of phases in two adjacent regions cannot be the same. Consider again the two-phase space composed of two phases, a and b, and assume that the neighboring space is constructed of two other phases—for example, a and c. It may now be asked how the process of getting from one state space into the other may be carried out. It could evidently be accomplished only by the simultaneous vanishing of b and appearance of c at the boundary. The appearance of c signifies that one phase—for example, melt—has become saturated in and has begun to precipitate out this phase. On the other hand, the disappearance of b indicates that as the alloy passed the boundary of the first two-phase space, the concentration of this phase was reduced below the saturation value. Hence, the conclusion is reached that along the surface of contact of the two state spaces the melt must be simultaneously saturated in two different phases; but the impossibility of such a case has already been demonstrated. These conclusions are generally valid. A phase space cannot be bounded by a second one containing the same number of phases.

It has already been mentioned that this analysis is limited by the highest number of phases prescribed by the phase rule. An invariant four-phase equilibrium can exist only on a plane at constant temperature. Hence, a four-phase space, which according to what has just been said must be bordered by a three-phase space, shrinks to a plane—for example, the plane of the ternary eutectic. This four-phase equilibrium plane must be bounded below by another three-phase space—in this case, the space of three solid phases. From this fact there exists a situation in which the three-phase spaces of binary eutectic crystallization seem to adjoin the three-phase space of solid substances along a surface. This apparent contradiction comes about through the existence of the plane of four-phase equilibrium between them. It is possible to formulate the relation-ship between phase spaces in such a way as to make an exception of three-phase regions separated by a horizontal plane.*

The above relationships are valid not only for three-component sys-tems, but generally.

A point of interest concerns the regions in the various plane sections previously described. These diagrams represent the intersection of planes with the different state spaces. Hence, the conclusions drawn concerning ternary diagrams must likewise be valid for all plane sections, both isothermal and perpendicular to the plane of concentration. A general examination of these various diagrams reveals their obedience to the above laws. Conversely, application of these principles serves as a method of testing the correctness of any particular section.

In any discussion of heterogeneous equilibria in multiple component systems, the above principles should always be kept in mind as a guide.

* Note by translator: The four-phase plane may be considered a degenerate four-phase space—that is, a four-phase space for which one dimension has decreased to zero.

Chapter III

Unbroken Solid Solution Series

If the binary systems which constitute the ternary system form unbroken series of solid solutions, then the latter may also be of this type over the whole of the concentration triangle. Such is not always the case, however, since gaps in solubility may occur within the ternary system. This possibility will be reserved for later discussion. Assume the simplest case—namely, that the binary solid solutions exhibit neither maximum nor minimum points (Figs. 23 and 24). The crystallization in such a

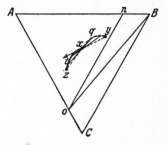

Fig. 23.

Triangle of concentrations of a system exhibiting complete miscibility in the solid state.

system proceeds in a manner very similar to that of a binary solid solution. From an alloy X, which at higher temperatures is a homogeneous liquid, there precipitates out, upon reaching the liquidus surface, a solid substance of composition Y different from X. At this moment the solid solution is in equilibrium with the melt X and the horizontal line combining X and Y is a conode (Fig. 24). Coincident with precipitation of this solid solution, the composition of the melt is displaced along the conode yx in the direction indicated by the arrow in Fig. 23. This fact is perceived at once from the following analysis: The total composition of the alloy is represented by the point x, which must always lie on the conode joining the compositions of the solid solution and the melt. Therefore, the composition of the melt is initially displaced in such a way that the line yx is tangent to the curve xtz at x. Usually, as the metal solidifies the curve xtz bends away from the projection of yx, and correspondingly yqx deviates from the line yx. During the entire process of freezing, the conodes specify the composition of the melt and the solid solution which are in equilibrium with each other. Throughout solidification, two phases exist

37

—the melt and the precipitated solid solution in equilibrium with it; therefore, from the phase rule, the system at constant pressure has two degrees of freedom. Correspondingly, the continuum of saturated melts (liquidus surface) must be represented geometrically by one continuous surface. Furthermore, since in contrast to the case considered in Chapter II, the composition of the solid solution varies continuously, the two-phase space must be bounded by a second continuous surface—namely, the surface of the solid solution in equilibrium with the melt (the solidus surface). As a rule, both surfaces are curved.

In a sense, the two-phase space of primary crystallization being considered here is a more general case of the type described in the previous chapter. The latter is obtained from the one now under discussion by noting that in consequence of the unchanging composition of the solid phase (pure component) the solidus surface shrinks to a point which may be considered as the perpendicular section of the prism edge.

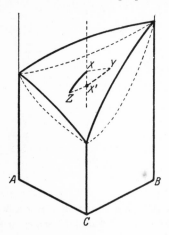

Fig. 24.

Space diagram of a system exhibiting complete miscibility in the solid state.

The solidification process is completed in a manner similar to that in a binary diagram. As the composition and temperature of the melt are displaced along the liquidus surface, and simultaneously more solid material is precipitated, the composition of the solid solution is displaced along the solidus surface through the mechanism of diffusion. As a consequence, the composition of the residual melt departs further and further from the mean composition, while that of the solid solution approaches the value for the alloy. When the composition of the solid phase has attained that of the alloy, the last drop of molten material will have become solid. The curve xz (Fig. 23) represents the continuum of compositions through which the melt passes during the process of solidification, and the curve yx, the continuum of compositions of solid solution. At the beginning of solidification the liquidus line starts to move away from the point x in the direction of the projection of the conode yx. Similarly, the solidus line finishes its motion at the point x while proceeding in the direction of the conode connecting the points x and z. This situation is visualized more easily if the reverse process of melting is considered. At the beginning of the melting process the solid solution has the composition of the alloy x. The first drop of liquid to be given off by the solid solution will have the composition z. Since the mean composition of the mixture of both phases must always be represented by the point x, it follows exactly as described above for the beginning of freezing that, as soon as the first liquid drop is given up, the composition of the solid solution x begins to move in the direction of the projection of the conode zx. The curves xz and yz are therefore the same for both the freezing and melting processes.

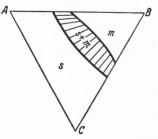

Fig. 25.

Isothermal section through the freezing range in a system exhibiting complete miscibility.

The conode connecting the two phases existing in equilibrium generates a kind of screw surface during the process of solidification. Its position remains horizontal with one end moving along the curve XZ (Fig. 24) while the other follows the curve YX. The screw-axis is the vertical line through the mean composition of the alloy, for all the conodes must pass through this point.

The space diagram breaks up into three partial spaces—the homogeneous space of the melt, the homogeneous space of the solid solution, and between them the two-phase space in which both the solid and liquid exist.

The form of the isothermal section in this case is very simple (Fig. 25). The two homogeneous areas of melt s and solid solution m are separated from each other by the two-phase band, in which the conodes have been drawn in schematically. These conodes differ from those described in the case of the mechanical mixture in not all being referred to a single point. For this reason their position cannot be specified from the concentration of the solidifying alloy, as was done in the previous chapter. They designate the solid solution and melt which are in equilibrium with each other at the temperature under consideration.

From the form of the ternary diagram it is possible to derive at once the nature of the vertical section. The cut *Bo* (Fig. 23) has the form shown in Fig. 26, and the section *on* is exhibited in Fig. 27. The differ-

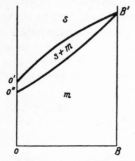

FIG. 26. Section *Bo* (Fig. 23).

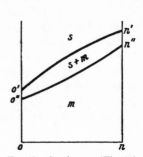

FIG. 27. Section *on* (Fig. 23).

ence between these diagrams and the diagram of a two-component system is obvious. Such forms are impossible in the latter case. The reason for this fundamental difference is that in a section of a ternary system, the conodes in general do not lie in the plane of the cut—a fact which is

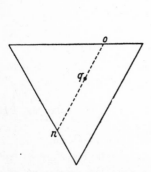

FIG. 28. Triangle of concentrations of a system with complete miscibility in the solid state and exhibiting a ternary maximum.

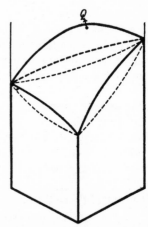

FIG. 29. Space diagram of a system with complete miscibility in the solid state and exhibiting a ternary maximum *Q*.

particularly evident at the sides of the cuts. Obviously the phases *o'* and *o''* are not in equilibrium with each other, nor are *n'* and *n''*, for in each case the corresponding phases are at different temperatures. The phase which is actually in equilibrium with o'' is a solid solution of A and C, of which the composition, as deduced from Figs. 23 and 24, lies between the points o and A. Similar considerations hold for the entire curves $o'n'$ and $o''n''$.

Just as in binary systems, there are ternary systems of the unbroken solid solution type in which the surface of the beginning of crystallization exhibits a maximum or a minimum. It can be rigorously shown that in such a case the surface of the end of crystallization also has a maximum

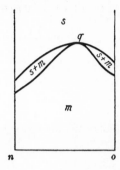

Fig. 30.

Section no (Fig. 28).

or a minimum at the same point and touches the liquidus surface there. These maxima and minima may exist in the component binary systems or simply within the ternary diagram. Such cases present nothing new. A system (Figs. 28 and 29) may have a maximum q (Q) inside the concentration triangle, and in this event will have a perpendicular section of the form nqo, as shown in Fig. 30. At the maximum the liquidus and solidus lines are in contact.

Chapter IV

System Having a Binary Compound with an Open Maximum but Without Formation of Solid Solution

A. System with Two Ternary Eutectics

1. Process of Crystallization

If compounds appear in a ternary system they may either lie entirely within the concentration triangle and hence be ternary compounds, or they may be binary compounds which originate in the binary systems and participate in the ternary system. A better designation than "com-

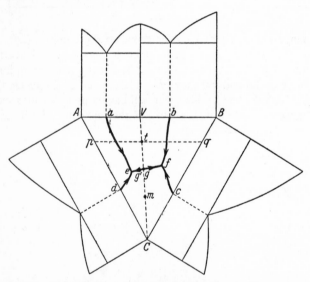

Fig. 31.   Triangle of concentrations in the case of a binary compound V with an open maximum.

pounds" for these molecular types would be "intermediate crystalline forms with restricted solid solution regions," because the theory of heterogeneous equilibrium tells nothing about the molecular structure of phases. However, it will be convenient in the following discussion to employ the less accurate nomenclature. Assume the case in which the system exhibits only one binary compound and no solid solutions occur. Fig. 31 shows the concentration triangle for such a system where one binary diagram *A-B* possesses a compound *V* with an open maximum.

When there is no formation of solid solution the solid portion of the ternary system breaks into two partial systems, *VBC* and *VAC*, separated from each other by the dotted line *V-C*. In the first system, all ternary alloys in the solid state consist of a mixture of the three crystalline types *V*, *B*, and *C*, and in the second of *V*, *A*, and *C*. This structure is the only possible one for the solid alloys for, according to the phase rule, only three crystalline forms may be present in any finite temperature interval, and the absence of the compound *V* in any of the alloys is not a possible exception so long as equilibrium conditions prevail, as has been assumed here.

The next question to present itself concerns the nature of the freezing process in alloys having such a constitution. The system possesses four binary eutectic points: *a*, *b*, *c*, and *d*. The simultaneous precipitation of two crystalline forms such as occurs at each of these eutectic points must take place at a lower temperature if there is an addition of a third substance, since the concentration in the melt of the phases crystallizing out is diminished thereby. In other words, the eutectic curves of doubly saturated melt which start out from each of these points must fall away to lower temperatures as they proceed toward the interior of the triangle to meet at some point. These intersections will next be considered. In general, the conditions here are quite similar to those in the case of ternary mechanical mixtures discussed in Chapter II.

Let us consider, for example, the curves of doubly saturated melt which extend out from *a* and *d*. They meet within the partial triangle *AVC* and at their intersection point, *e*, the melt is in equilibrium with the three crystalline forms *A*, *C*, and *V*. There occurs therefore an invariant, four-phase situation which can exist at only one temperature and one composition of the melt and in which, as explained in Chapter I, two kinds of reactions may occur upon the withdrawal of heat. If, as in the present case, one of the phases participating in this equilibrium lies within the triangle formed by the other three, then the reaction which takes place is that the one phase (melt) disappears into the other three; or, conversely, if heat is added, the amount of the one phase increases at the expense of the other three. The reaction is

$$\text{melt } e \rightleftarrows A + C + V. \tag{1}$$

The other possibility, as discussed in Chapter I, is that two phases react with each other to produce two other phases. A necessary condition for this type of reaction is that none of the participating phases have a composition which lies within the triangle formed by the other three (in this case, *A*, *V*, and *C*). (1) is the equation of a ternary eutectic reaction. It indicates how the solidification process is completed at the ternary eutectic point where the melt has the composition e. A third curve of doubly saturated melt must also intersect at this point. The melt of this third curve must be in equilibrium with the two crystalline forms V and C.

A quite similar behavior takes place in the partial triangle VBC if the assumption is made that the two curves, bf and cf, of binary eutectic crystallization which extend out from points b and c intersect within the partial triangle at f, as shown in Fig. 31. This intersection point is likewise a ternary eutectic point into which must run a third curve of doubly saturated melt which is in equilibrium with V and C.

It will be seen that in the two partial triangles there are, respectively, the binary eutectic curves ge and gf, along which the same phases, melt and the two crystalline forms V and C, are in equilibrium. They differ from each other only in the different composition of the liquid phase. The melts having compositions on the curve ge belong to the system AVC and obviously lie within the triangle AVC. Melts on gf belong to the system BVC and lie within that triangle. These two curves must meet in a binary eutectic point in which the two substances, V and C, crystallize out without excess of either A or B—that is, in the point g on the line VC. It is a simple matter to show that this point must correspond to the highest temperature to be found along the curve egf. First, there is the consideration which has already been applied to binary eutectic points at the sides of a concentration triangle—namely, that through the addition of A or B the amounts of the crystallizing phase V and C in the melt are decreased; hence the temperature of crystallization must fall. This argument is not completely conclusive, however, for in ternary melts equilibrium situations and states of dissociation of a complicated type may occur which are not readily perceived. In fact, it will later be seen that there are cases where such a simple analysis does not hold.

Other arguments of a simple kind may be presented. Let it be assumed that the maximum of the curve egf' does not occur at g but at some point, g', to the left of g. It may first be assumed that in the interval $g'g$ the composition of the melt is displaced in the direction from g' to g. However, since V and C are being precipitated, the melt must become continually richer in A, and therefore its representative point must actually proceed in the opposite direction. This assumption having been shown to give rise to an impossible situation, it may next be assumed that the melt actually does go from g toward g' as V and C solidify out. In this case the temperature must rise, since g' has been taken to be the maximum temperature in the interval $g'g$. As a consequence, the temperature of the alloy must rise during this stage of solidification; but such a situation cannot occur under equilibrium conditions. Hence, the second assumption is also unjustifiable. Therefore, no other point except *g* can be the maximum.

The alloys with compositions lying in the cut *VC* crystallize exactly in the same manner as in a binary system. The liquid alloys do not leave the concentrations represented by the section *VC* during the whole crystallization process. To demonstrate this fact convincingly, let us consider the solidification of some alloy *m* (Fig. 31). The crystalline *C* is precipitated from it and the composition of the melt is displaced in the direction of the arrow *Cm* passing through *C* and the point *m*. This arrow obviously lies along the line *VC*, and hence during the process of primary crystallization the melt remains entirely on this line. Upon reaching the binary eutectic point *g*, the composition of the melt cannot

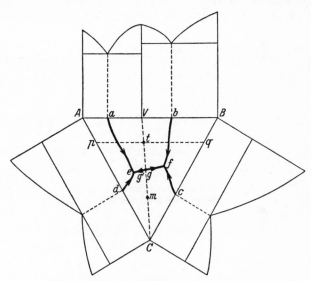

Fig. 31.   Triangle of concentrations in the case of a binary compound *V* with an open maximum.

proceed any farther toward *V*, but remains on the line *VC*. The solidification of all alloys of the section *VC* follows exactly as for a binary alloy, and in no instance does the behavior of an alloy give any indication that it is a member of a ternary system. Such sections lying within a system of higher order but behaving like a binary alloy system are called "quasi-binary sections."

Let us continue to assume that there are two ternary eutectic points, *e* and *f*, lying within the triangles *AVC* and *VBC*, and hence that *VC* is a quasi-binary section. The complete ternary system breaks up during the process of solidification into two partial systems, *AVC* and *BVC*, each of which represents the simple case of a mechanical mixture as described in Chapter II. It is therefore necessary only to consider the details of solidification by referring to that chapter. The processes which occur here may be considered as those of two simple systems with eutectics, which lie side by side in just the same way as in a binary system with an open maximum.

The partial ternary systems show a difference when compared with two complete ternary systems which is very similar to the one demonstrated by the two parts of a complete binary system. In the latter case the liquidus curve makes a definite angle with the horizontal as it leaves the pure components, as will be observed for the systems *A-B* and *B-C* in Fig. 31. For the partial systems of *A-B* it will be perceived that the liquidus line shows no discontinuity at *V*, but forms a maximum with a horizontal tangent and hence is mathematically continuous. Likewise,

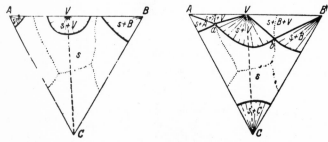

Figs. 32 and 33. Isothermal sections in the case of a compound *V* which gives rise to a quasi-binary section *VC*.

the liquidus surface of a ternary system shows no discontinuity where it crosses the quasi-binary cut. This difference, concerning which no further explanation will be given, depends on the fact that in the melt a partial dissociation of the compound occurs in which $V \rightleftharpoons A + B$.

It need scarcely be said that this problem has nothing to do with the phase rule or the theory of heterogeneous equilibria, since the question here is one of homogeneous equilibrium within a phase.

2. Isothermal Sections

In Figs. 32-34 several isothermal cuts in the freezing range of the system are presented. As is customary, the regions of primary crystallization are indicated by a system of conodes which connect the precipitated solid with the corresponding melt. Fig. 32 represents the situation after the primary crystallization of *A*, *V*, and *B* has begun, but before binary eutectic crystallization occurs. Within the regions of primary crystallization $s+A$, $s+V$, and $s+B$, the alloys consist of mixtures of crystals and their corresponding melts. In the remaining portion of the system there is only the homogeneous melt s.

Fig. 33 corresponds to a temperature for which the binary eutectic crystallization of A and V and of V and B has set in. Hence there will be, in addition to the regions of primary crystallization indicated by conodes, the areas $s+A+V$ and $s+B+V$ within which the alloy members consist of melt and two crystalline types. On the basis of the discussion given in Chapter II, it is self-evident that on isothermal sections the lines separating regions of primary and binary eutectic crystallization must appear as straight lines, since they represent intersections of a horizontal plane with a surface which was generated through the motion of a horizontal line. The compositions of the melts a and b, with each of which two crystalline forms are in equilibrium, lie on the dotted curves. It is scarcely necessary to mention that these curves do not lie in the section under consideration but only intersect it at the points a and b.

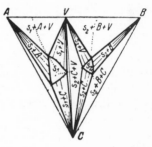

Fig. 34.

Isothermal sections in the case of a compound V which gives rise to a quasi-binary section VC.

A later stage of solidification is shown in Fig. 34. All of the binary eutectic points of the system have been encountered, and instead of four, there are now six regions of primary crystallization in which the four crystalline types A, V, B, and C appear. This condition arises from the fact that the compound V and the component C have a region of primary crystallization in each of the partial systems AVC and VBC. These partial regions of crystallization produce the same crystalline forms but are separated from each other near the section VC by regions of binary eutectic solidification. There are also six areas of binary eutectic crystallization corresponding to the two partial systems into which the complete ternary system divides and two regions of homogeneous melt, s_1 and s_2.

3. Vertical Sections

Of the sections perpendicular to the plane of concentration we shall consider only the cut pq (see Figs. 31 and 35). A complete discussion of this section is not necessary, since it is simply a combination of two sections of the type discussed in Chapter II. The curve abc has a maximum at the composition of the point t (Fig. 31), since b must be a point in the quasi-binary section previously mentioned. The curves ab and bc lie outside of the cut pq and form the continuum of the points of intersection of the vertical plane with the conodes joining the curves eg and gf with V. On the other hand, the curve of the beginning of crystallization dS_1f is composed of points which lie in the section. Its maximum,

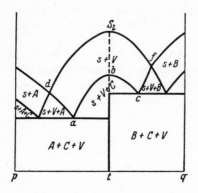

Fig. 35.

Section pq (Fig. 31).

S_1, need not, however, correspond to the composition of the point t. Whether it does or not depends upon the angle between the sections VC and pq. In the general case, it is improbable that such correspondence will occur.

B. System with a Ternary Eutectic and a Ternary Peritectic

1. Process of Crystallization

It is not necessary, as we have hitherto assumed, that the intersection point of two binary eutectic curves shall lie inside of the partial triangle in which they originate—for example, it is quite possible that the intersection point e of ae and de may lie within the triangle VBC, as illustrated in Fig. 36. Since the melt represented by ae is saturated in A and V and the liquid alloy corresponding to de is saturated in A and C, the melt e is simultaneously saturated in A, C, and the compound V. Hence, the situation at e must be that of invariant equilibrium. As the point e does not lie within the triangle formed by the three solid phases, the present arrangement cannot correspond to a eutectic reaction similar to (1) but to one of the type

$$A + \text{melt } e \rightleftharpoons V + C \tag{2}$$

Consider the special case of an alloy composed of A and e in such proportions that its average composition is n; then the amounts of V and C formed by reaction (2) will be such that their average composition also corresponds to the point n. The latter is the intersection point of the two lines Ae and VC. A reaction of the type given in (2) is called a "peritectic reaction," and e is a ternary peritectic point.

If the composition of the alloy lies within the triangle AVC, then melt e will be consumed by reaction (2) until it disappears, and only the three crystal types A, V, and C remain—that is, the solidification process comes to an end at this point. On the other hand, if the composition of the alloy lies to the right of the line VC, the constituent A will all be consumed by reaction with the melt at e and only the three phases V, C, and melt e will remain.

Corresponding to the existence of three phases V, C, and e, there will be one degree of freedom. Hence, the temperature and the compositions of the phases participating in the equilibrium may undergo a change. The alloys within the triangle AVC are not concerned by this condition, since for these all the melt is consumed at e and the composition of the crystalline forms has been assumed not to change with temperature. If

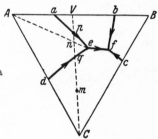

Fig. 36.

Binary compound V without a quasi-binary section VC.

the alloy lies to the right of the line VC then V, C, and and the melt remain, the last being saturated in both of the solid substances. While further precipitation takes place the composition of the residual melt is displaced to the right—that is, farther away from the line VC—and simultaneously the temperature drops. This behavior signifies that besides the two curves ae and de a third curve, ef, intersects at e. This curve runs to lower temperatures as it leaves e.

Later discussion (Chapter V) will show that binary eutectic and peritectic solidifications in ternary systems are not mutually exclusive as they are in the binary case, but that the former type of crystallization can transform continuously into the latter. If an invariant equilibrium exists, as when one liquid and three solid phases are present, this transition from one type of solidification to the other cannot take place. In this case, the reaction can proceed only eutectically according to (1), or peritectically according to (2). The two types of solidification are mutually exclusive and a transformation from one type into the other does not occur.

After the substance A has been consumed at the peritectic point e, the solidification of the alloy proceeds by further precipitation of V and C, during which the composition of the melt moves along the curve ef. The melt is constantly enriched in B and eventually becomes saturated in this constituent. There will then be present besides the liquid, the three solid substances V, B, and C, so that an invariant equilibrium again exists; in this instance it is a eutectic equilibrium, since the composition of melt f lies inside the triangle VBC formed by the three crystalline substances. It need scarcely to be stated that two additional curves of binary eutectic crystallization bf and cf must intersect at the point f. All compositions in the partial system VBC complete their solidification at this point.

In spite of the difference in the process of freezing of the alloys, the state of the system after solidification is the same as in the case previously considered. However, this statement is valid only if during the solidification process there has been no departure from the equilibrium state, an assumption which, as is well known, is seldom fulfilled for peritectic reactions under usual cooling conditions.

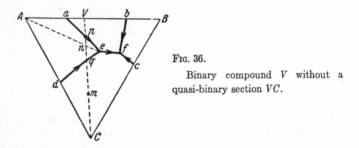

Fig. 36.

Binary compound V without a quasi-binary section VC.

In the case just described, the line VC does not correspond to a quasi-binary section, for the composition of the melt does not remain in the section during solidification. Consider for example an alloy m (Fig. 36). Its solidification begins by precipitation of the substance C from the melt. The composition of the melt is therefore displaced in the direction from m toward q. As soon as q is reached the melt becomes saturated in A, not in V as in the previous case. As a result, the binary eutectic crystallization of A and C begins and the composition of the melt leaves the binary cut VC to follow the curve qe. For the alloys of the part Vp a similar procedure takes place; the composition of the melt, upon reaching p after primary precipitation of the compound V, follows along the curve pe. In the part pq solidification begins with the primary crystallization of A and the composition of the melt moves along the direction of the line coming from A. The behavior in such a system may be characterized by saying that the compound V which forms an open maximum in the binary system is partially transformed in the ternary system into the case of a concealed maximum.

The behavior which has just been described is more complicated than in the simple system first discussed. Hence, it is profitable to study the course of solidification by means of sections.

2. Isothermal Sections

After the primary solidification has begun, there is a period when the crystallization of A, V, and B has set in but no C has been formed. This stage is quite like that shown in Fig. 32. Besides the region of the melt there are at the given temperature, three areas of primary crystallization within which the alloys consist of a mixture of melt and solid constituent.

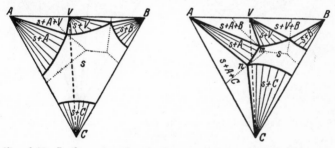

FIGS. 37 and 38. Isothermal sections in the case of a compound V without a quasi-binary section VC.

At lower temperatures—that is, below the binary eutectic points a and b —Fig. 37 is obtained. This diagram differs only to a slight degree from the one shown in Fig. 33 for approximately the same temperature. As in Fig. 33, there are two ternary fields of binary eutectic crystallization, $s+A+V$ and $s+V+B$. The principal difference is that in Fig. 37 the region $s+A$ of primary crystallization extends itself more rapidly and has almost reached the binary cut VC.

For temperatures below the binary eutectic point d (Fig. 36), the conditions are as shown in Fig. 38. The point m of binary eutectic crystallization of A and V has already passed beyond the line VC. The region of homogeneous melt s has been reduced and a new area, $s+A+C$, of binary eutectic crystallization of A and C has come into existence as the result of the section dropping below the temperature of the eutectic d in the side AC. The assumption is made here that the temperature of the binary eutectic point, c, on the side BC has not yet been passed.

As the horizontal section descends to the temperature of the peritectic point, e (Fig. 39), the points corresponding to m and n in Fig. 38 coincide with e and the triangle Amn shrinks to the straight line Ae. The solid A can now exist in equilibrium with only one composition of liquid phase— namely, the peritectic melt e. The line Ae is the line of intersection of the two screw-type surfaces which form the upper boundaries of the spaces of binary eutectic crystallization of A and V in one case and of A and C in the other (see Fig. 11, line LG''').

Since the temperature now being considered still lies above the eutectic point in the binary system BC, the residual region, s, of the homogeneous melt still extends to the side of the triangle which corresponds to this binary system. For all temperatures below the peritectic point, e, the behavior differs from that just described in that the solid A can no longer

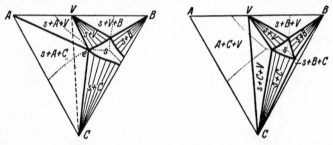

Figs. 39 and 40. Isothermal sections in the case of a compound V without a quasi-binary section. VC.

exist along with the melt. This condition arises, as will be seen in Fig. 40, from the fact that all alloys within the partial triangle AVC have now solidified. The solidification process is unfinished only for the alloys of the partial triangle VBC. Hence from this point on, the diagram corresponds to the process in a simple mechanical mixture which has already been described in connection with Fig. 17 and needs no further discussion. The reader therefore need give no further consideration to the isothermal sections at lower temperatures.

3. Vertical Sections

Of the possible sections perpendicular to the plane of concentration we shall consider mn, op, qr, and At, as illustrated in Fig. 41. The first three are parallel to the side AB of the triangle. The cut mn is shown in Fig. 42. This section shows that three different kinds of primary solidification take place. From m to g, the solid A (Fig. 41) is thrown out; from g to l, the solid V; and from l to n, the solid B. Hence, the curve of the beginning of crystallization (Fig. 42) may be considered to consist of three different portions which join one another. For the alloys of the interval *me'* (Fig. 41) the primary crystallization of *A* is followed by the crystallization of the binary eutectic *A+C*. The temperature of the beginning of this binary eutectic crystallization becomes lower as the percentage of *B* in the melt increases (curve *m'e'*, Fig. 42). For the alloy *e'* the ternary peritectic point, *e*, is reached directly at the conclusion of the primary crystallization of *A*. Alloys of the segment *e'g* (Fig. 41) undergo the binary eutectic crystallization of *A+V* upon the completion of the primary precipitation of *A*. Those belonging to *gh'* also precipitate out *V* and *A* simultaneously as soon as the primary crystallization of *V* has been concluded. All the alloys which have been considered here reach the ternary peritectic point, *e*, at the conclusion of the binary eutectic crystallization process. Since an invariant equilibrium exists at *e*, the peritectic reaction occurs here for all alloys at the constant temperature of the horizontal line *m''e'h'* (Fig. 42).

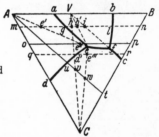

Fig. 41.

Position of sections *mn, op, qr,* and
At.

The alloys of the interval *h'i* experience a binary eutectic crystallization of *V* and *C* as soon as the primary crystallization of *V* has been completed (*h'f*, Fig. 42). In the section *i* to *l*, compound *V* is first precipitated, followed by the simultaneous formation of *V+B* (*fl*, Fig. 42). In segment *ln*, *B* comes out first and at the end of this process is formed one of the binary eutectics *V+B* or *B+C*.

Although the solidification of alloys in the interval *mh* is completed by the peritectic reaction because all the melt has been consumed during the process, in part *hi* some liquid alloy still remains after the completion of the peritectic reaction which consumed all the crystals of *A*. Hence, there follows a binary eutectic crystallization of *V* and *C* together, as will be seen in Fig. 42. For the alloys to the right of *h'* (Fig. 41) the peritectic reaction does not occur.

Solidification of all alloys to the right of point *h* is finished during the ternary eutectic crystallization which occurs when the composition of the melt reaches *f*.

Consideration of the section *op* (Fig. 41) shows that the diagram

(Fig. 43) has been only slightly displaced. The only marked difference between the two figures is that the intersection point, g, of the curves of primary crystallization of A and V lies to the right of the perpendicular section VC. Also the alloy e'', which lies on the line Ae, is to the right of the line VC (e'', Fig. 43). Correspondingly, the limiting composition for which the solidification is finished in the ternary eutectic point f lies to the left of the point e''.

If Figs. 42 and 43 are compared with the corresponding case illustrated in Fig. 35, it will be seen that 42, and even more so 43, indicate a concealed maximum and a peritectic reaction. This situation will be made clear in the next section.

The cut qr is different from those hitherto considered because no primary crystallization of the compound V occurs (Fig. 44). For the alloys in the interval from q to d', primary crystallization is followed by precipitation of the binary eutectic $A+C$ (curve $q''d'$). To the left of VC (Fig. 41), the crystallization process is completed by the peritectic reaction. In the alloys between the section VC and the point e''' the

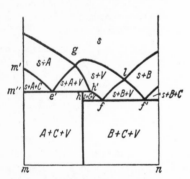

Fig. 42. Section mn (Fig. 41).

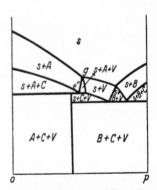

Fig. 43. Section op (Fig. 41).

binary eutectic crystallization of V and C occurs after the completion of the peritectic reaction. Solidification of all alloys to the right of the line VC is completed at the ternary eutectic point. Examination shows that the cut VC has no particular relation to the primary and binary eutectic crystallization lines. It is only in the solid state that it provides the boundary between the three-phase spaces $A+V+C$ and $B+V+C$. Regarding the form of the regions $s+A$, $s+B$, $s+A+C$, and $s+B+C$, the considerations are the same as those mentioned in connection with Fig. 22a.

The cut At (Fig. 41) has a comparatively simple form. The curve of the beginning of crystallization consists of the two parts, au and ut (Fig. 45). Along the first curve primary crystallization of A occurs, and along the second the element C is precipitated. It is at once obvious that the binary eutectic crystallization of A and C in part Au (Fig. 41) must begin at constant temperature, exactly as described in the case of Fig. 19 (line $a'u$, Fig. 45). The same binary eutectic crystallization also occurs in the interval uw, this time at the close of the primary precipitation of C. The point w lies on the line Ce. For all alloys of the part Aw there occurs at the conclusion of the binary eutectic crystalliza-

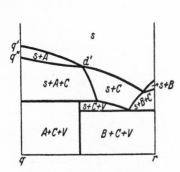

FIG. 44. Section qr (Fig. 41).

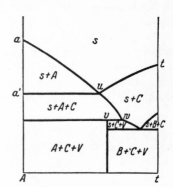

FIG. 45. Section At (Fig. 41).

tion the ternary peritectic reaction in which the melt has the composition of the point e. For the alloys of the interval wt, this peritectic reaction no longer takes place. For the alloys within the partial triangle AVC—that is, from A to v in the cut At—the process of solidification is brought to a close during the peritectic reaction. For the alloys of the part vt, freezing is completed at the ternary eutectic point f.

C. An Impossible Constitutional Case

We may propose to ourselves the question whether besides the two types of solidification which have been discussed there is another possibility, still maintaining the assumption that the compound V forms an open maximum. Hitherto, consideration has been given only to the case in which the curves extending out from the binary eutectic points a and d on the one hand and b and c on the other (Figs. 31 and 36) intersect each other to form either a ternary eutectic or a ternary peritectic point. An examination should now be made of the possibility that a different behavior may occur and that curves going out from a and b meet, as do likewise those extending out from c and d. It is evident that the first condition requires the second to be true.

Let it be assumed that the conditions are as illustrated in Fig. 46. The curve ae of melt simultaneously saturated in A and V and the curve be, which is the path of the liquid saturated in V and B, meet in the point e. At this point there is an invariant equilibrium with the four phases A, V, B, and melt e. Hence, all concentrations are fixed and the reaction which occurs can affect only the amounts of the phases under consideration. A little thought shows that such a reaction is not possible. The melt cannot solidify eutectically for it would have to break up into the three solid phases, A, V, and B, a condition which is impossible according to the specified concentrations, for the composition of the liquid would have to lie inside of the triangle whose corners are the concentrations of the three given solid forms. Furthermore, a peritectic reaction is also impossible because the four points A, V, B, and e would have to form a quadrangle without re-entrant angles. Since all three solid phases lie on one side, AB, of the triangle, the only reaction which could take place would be one in the binary system AB involving the breaking up of the compound V according to the reaction $V \rightleftharpoons A + B$.

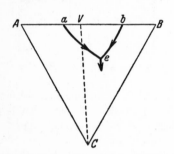

FIG. 46. Impossible manner of freezing in the case of a binary compound.

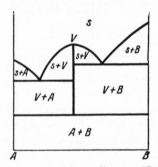

FIG. 46a. The binary diagram AB for the freezing process shown in Fig. 46.

In this case the diagram AB takes on the form shown in Fig. 46a. The intersection of the curves ae and be (Fig. 46) lies at the temperature of the breaking up of compound V in the binary system. This fact might at first be considered accidental, but the situation could not be otherwise. As soon as the compound V has split up there can no longer be two binary eutectic curves. These must have joined and their junction must have occurred at the temperature of the breaking up of compound V and the point e. If the binary compound does not break up but remains stable at low temperature, as was assumed at the beginning of the chapter, the path of the binary eutectic curves shown in Fig. 46 represents an impossible case.

The above analysis is valid only as long as there is no formation of solid solution in the solid state. Let it now be assumed that the three crystal forms A, V, and B exist in the limited homogeneous regions α, γ, and β, respectively, as shown in Fig. 47 (the boundary of the solid solution regions may be assumed to be independent of the temperature). Then the composition of the solid solution γ existing in equilibrium with the melt is in general not on the straight line connecting the constituents α and β which also participate in this equilibrium. According to the location of the lines combining γ with the other constituents, either a eutectic or a peritectic case will exist. If the lines are situated as shown in Fig. 47, the invariant reaction will be of the peritectic type: melt $e + \gamma \rightleftarrows \alpha + \beta$. If γ lies at a re-entrant angle the reaction will be of the eutectic type: $\gamma \rightleftarrows \alpha + \beta + $ melt e. In neither case can the solid solution γ be in equilibrium with the melt below the temperature of the point e.

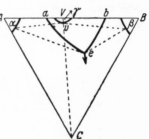

FIG. 47.

The freezing process of Fig. 46 becomes possible if limited solid solution formation occurs.

It is evident therefore that the processes of solidification illustrated in Figs. 31 and 36 and discussed in sections A and B represent the only possible arrangements for a binary compound with an open maximum.

D. Two Compounds. The Klarkreuz Method of W. Guertler

Let us now consider a system with two binary compounds V_1 and V_2, as illustrated in Fig. 48. In the simplest structural case, these compounds behave as simple components—that is, the ternary system is divided by quasi-binary sections into ternary sub-systems of the type which form simple mechanical mixtures with eutectics. This problem corresponds to the one discussed in section A. Let it be assumed that the system of Fig. 48 is divided in a similar manner. - It will be noticed that such a division is possible in two ways: either into the partial systems AV_1V_2, V_1V_2B, and V_2BC, or into the combination AV_1V_2, V_1V_2C, and V_1BC. In the first case, V_2B is a quasi-binary cut and in the second, V_1C. In the former division, the compound V_1 cannot exist together with C, whereas V_2 and B can coexist; in the second, V_2 cannot exist simultaneously with B but V_1 and C may occur together. Between the two possibilities rather important structural differences exist.

Since, according to the phase rule, only three different crystalline forms may exist simultaneously in a phase space in which the temperature varies, only one of the two possible alternative types can occur.

Hence, this conclusion is quite independent of whether any of the vertical cuts V_1C, V_2B, and V_2V_1 behave as quasi-binary sections during the freezing process. It should be emphasized that the present discussion is concerned only with the solid state, and also that it is rigorously correct.

Guertler[1] developed his Klarkreuz method for making a preliminary test of the type of ternary system being examined under the assumption that solidification takes place in the simplest way with the formation of quasi-binary sections. Consider a system like that shown in Fig. 48, in which the two compounds, V_1 and V_2, occur in the binary systems. Both of the two possible types are constructed. Then instead of proceeding as formerly to the study of a more or less random series of compositions, the alloy of composition x which lies at the intersection of the lines V_1C and V_2B is examined first. If the crystal types V_1, C, V_2, and B are known, it is possible to determine immediately by examination whether

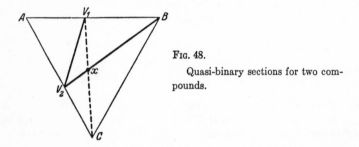

Fig. 48.

Quasi-binary sections for two compounds.

the structure is composed of crystals of V_1 and C or of V_2 and B. In doubtful cases, the investigation may be supplemented by examining a number of alloys along the lines V_1C and V_2B, and from a knowledge of their method of solidification as revealed by structural features, noting whether V_1C or V_2B is the quasi-binary section.

This ingenious method gives a conclusive answer when the constitutional case is the one described under A (eutectics only). It fails, however, for case B—that is, if the portion V_2V_1BC involves ternary peritectic reactions as well as eutectic ones. Experience has shown that peritectic reactions so seldom run to completion that the structural investigation of the alloy having composition x does not give definite results. Furthermore, it is not possible to establish which section is the quasi-binary one, because neither V_1C nor V_2B is necessarily of this type. Under such circumstances, the Klarkreuz method must be abandoned and recourse had to the usual procedure of a complete investigation of the system.

While the Klarkreuz method does seem to be limited, a trial is recommended in all cases in which its application appears possible. If it is successful, the investigation will be much shortened. If difficulties are encountered it is always possible to proceed to the usual systematic studies.

Further consideration of systems with multiple compounds but without solid solution formation appears superfluous, since no fundamentally new constitutional cases arise, although the complications may increase. This statement holds also if a ternary compound appears. For this reason, ternary compounds will not be treated in this book.

Chapter V

Solid Solutions with Solubility Breaks in Two Binary Systems

A. Eutectic Case

1. Process of Crystallization. State Spaces

The state diagrams which have hitherto been discussed may be rigorously derived from thermodynamic reasoning; particularly is it true that if the type of diagram of the ternary system is known, the general form

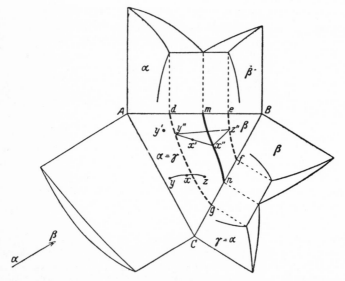

Fig. 49. Triangle of concentrations in the case of two eutectic solubility gaps in the solid state.

of the equilibrium surfaces and the equilibrium spaces are predictable. Under no circumstances, however, can the constitution of the ternary system be predicted from the diagrams of the binary systems from which it is formed. For this reason we shall generally limit ourselves to the consideration of the simplest or most illustrative cases.

The above comments are valid also for all the further cases considered in this book. As the complexity of the system grows, the number of possible assumptions, compatible with the given binary systems, which may be made concerning the constitution of the ternary system increases continously. In general we shall be concerned only with illustrative cases and shall not attempt to exhaust all the thermodynamically permissible possibilities. To do so would be extraordinarily difficult.

Consider the system indicated in Fig. 49 in which the two binary systems A-B and B-C possess solid solutions with miscibility gaps, whereas the third system, A-C, exhibits complete solubility. Let it be assumed that within the ternary system no new type of crystal is formed and that the gap in solubility extends completely through the ternary system. The latter assumption is not necessarily true, since such a gap may close within the ternary system; but discussion of such an example will be deferred until later (Chapter VIII).

The following facts concerning the form of the ternary space diagram shown in Fig. 49 may be stated immediately. Since the miscibility gaps in the solid state do not close within the system, there must be some internal connection between the two binary systems which display this characteristic. Furthermore, this connection must not encounter the side AC; otherwise a miscibility gap would appear in the system A-C, in contradiction to the original assumption. Hence, there must be regions of homogeneous solid solution α and β extending out respectively from the side AC and the corner B. In the simplest case, the boundaries of solid solution regions at the finish of solidification are the dotted curves dg and ef. Since only two types of crystalline material appear in the whole system, the occurrence of either a ternary eutectic or a ternary peritectic point is impossible, and the freezing process must come to an end without encountering such a reaction. The two eutectic points of the binary systems must be connected by a continuous curve mn. The limits of composition of the saturated solid solutions in the ternary systems will generally change with temperature in much the same manner as in binary systems. For this reason the solubility changes in the three-component system will not be considered. It is obvious that the curves dg and ef in Fig. 49 correspond to the limit of solubility only at the end of the freezing process. Since the solid solution γ in the system CB passes continuously into the solid solution α in the system AB, the entire region will be designated as α.

In the simplest case, the liquidus surface has the form given in Fig. 50. It falls continuously from the side AB toward the side BC and has in intermediate regions a eutectic depression MN, which drops away to lower temperatures in going from M toward N. In these remarks, the assumption has been made that the system AB melts at a higher temperature than the system BC, as depicted in Figs. 49 and 50.

The freezing of the homogeneous areas $AdgC$ and Bfe of the concentration triangle proceeds in the same way as in the previously considered problem of complete solid solubility described in Chapter III. Consider the solidification of an alloy of the composition x (Fig. 49). Upon reaching the liquidus surface a crystal of composition y is precipitated out. During freezing, the compositions of the melt and the solid follow along the curves xz and yx, respectively. Before the melt z has reached the curve of doubly saturated liquid mn, the composition of the solid solution has reached the composition of the point x, which means that solidification has been completed. The path indicating the course of solidification corresponds in all details to that described in Figs. 23 and 24 of Chapter III.

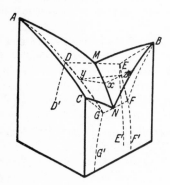

Fig. 50.

Schematic space diagram in the case of two eutectic solubility gaps in the solid state.

Conditions differ for the solidification of an alloy of which the composition lies within the miscibility break $defg$. For such an alloy, crystallization cannot be completed in a homogeneous manner. As an example, let us consider the solidification of an alloy x' (Fig. 49). Freezing will begin with the precipitation of a solid solution, y', in the same way as it does in a homogeneous portion, but before all the liquid has been consumed the composition of the solid has reached the bounding curve dg at the point y''. The fact that the solid solution y'' is saturated signifies that there must be a second phase with which it stands in equilibrium—in this instance, the solid solution z''. The liquid is therefore saturated in both α and β solid solutions as soon as the composition of the α solid solution has reached the point y'', and consequently throws out also β solid solution of composition z''. Hence, there sets in a period of binary eutectic crystallization which differs from the previously described process of this type only because the composition of the crystalline substance changes. The composition of the liquid must now be at the point x'' on the curve mn of doubly saturated melt. At this stage the saturated solid solution y'', the melt x'', and the average composition x' lie on a straight line, for the alloy consists of two phases, y'' and x'', the amount of the third phase z'' as yet being infinitely small.

As soon as the precipitation of the third phase has begun, the system is composed of three phases and possesses one degree of freedom. This condition implies that the compositions of the three participating phases lie on definite space curves, as previously discussed for the melt in a binary eutectic solidification. The saturation curve for the melt is mn; for the solid solution α ($=\gamma$) the saturation curve is dg; and for the solid solution β, ef.

The three phases define a concentration triangle $y''z''x''$ similar to the triangle of the binary eutectic crystallization of mechanical mixtures described in Chapter II. In that chapter it was shown that the composition of a melt moves along the curve of doubly saturated liquid, while the compositions of the crystalline materials remain unchanged since only pure components are precipitated. In such a system the solidification process cannot be completed with the precipitation of only two kinds of crystalline materials, for then the concentration point, x',

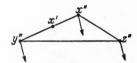

Fig. 51. Change of concentrations for an eutectic three-phase reaction.

Fig. 51a. An impossible arrangement for the case shown in Fig. 51.

of the whole alloy would necessarily have to lie on the conode connecting the two crystalline materials α and β. So long as the compositions of the two solid substances are fixed—for example, at the corners of the concentration triangle—this condition cannot be satisfied; hence crystallization must be completed by the precipitation of a third solid constituent having a composition such that it forms with the first two a triangle within which x' is located. It is obvious that the third component, C, satisfies this condition for the systems discussed in Chapter II.

In the case now under consideration the compositions of the two crystalline types, y'' and z'', which are in equilibrium with the melt x'' can also vary. Freezing proceeds in such a way that the entire triangle $y''x''z''$ is displaced, during further crystallization, to lower temperatures in the direction toward higher concentration of C along the curves dg, mn, and ef.

As previously mentioned, the composition of the alloy (point x', Fig. 51) lies, in the beginning, on one side of the triangle outlined by the three phases, because at this time the quantity of z'' present is infinitely small. As freezing continues, the compositions of the three phases are displaced by the processes of precipitation and diffusion along the saturation curves in the direction of the arrows to points indicated by the position of the dotted triangle. After this displacement, x' will be found in the interior of the triangle. The relative amounts of the two crystal types and liquid metal existing at any given time during the solidification period may be determined by the application of the center of gravity rule (Chapter I). As soon as the compositions, y'' and z'', of the two solid solutions have been displaced so far that the point x' lies on the conode connecting them, the amount of melt x'' must have decreased to zero, thus bringing the solidification process to a close. The result is a mixture of two solid solutions $\alpha\ (=\gamma)$ and β. It will be seen that solidification comes to an end for alloys within the portion *efgd* (Fig. 49) of the system, without any of the phases attaining a composition corresponding to a point on *BC*.

During solidification the horizontal triangle $y''z''x''$ is displaced to lower temperatures, thus generating a three-cornered, tube-like space which differs from that illustrated in Fig. 12 by having its back side also displaced. This three-phase space may be considered to originate at

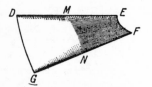

FIG. 52.

Three-phase space of binary eutectic crystallization.

the horizontal eutectic line of the binary system *AB*, extend into the interior of the system as a three-cornered tube, and end at the horizontal line of the eutectic arrest in the system *BC*. The shrinking of the tube to a line at the sides of the concentration triangle corresponds to the decreased number of degrees of freedom in the two-component systems. The form of the tube is indicated schematically in Fig. 52.

A little consideration will show that if the arrangement of the space diagram is like that shown in Fig. 50—that is, with the temperature of the beginning of crystallization decreasing toward the reader—then the concentration point x'' of the melt must always be in advance of y'' and z''. In other words the concentrations of the three participating phases y'', z'', and x'' are displaced, during the binary eutectic crystallization, in the direction of decreasing temperature, hence in the direction of the arrows in Fig. 51. Such a position of the triangle as shown in Fig. 51a is impossible because then the triangle cannot move to bring x' into its interior, a condition which is essential if the alloy is to consist of the three phases y'', x'', and z''.

The alloys having compositions on the curve *mn* begin the binary eutectic crystallization immediately upon starting to solidify. In the present case the binary eutectic crystallization differs from the similar process in a two-component system because of the new state region which comes into existence. Beginners frequently fail to note this difference and are inclined to assume that in the ternary system the three phases which are in equilibrium—that is, the melt x'' and the two solid solutions y'' and z''—all lie on a conode. If this idea were correct, the three-cornered space would shrink to a surface generated by the motion of a horizontal line. As a consequence, the binary eutectic crystallization of any given alloy within the ternary system would necessarily take place

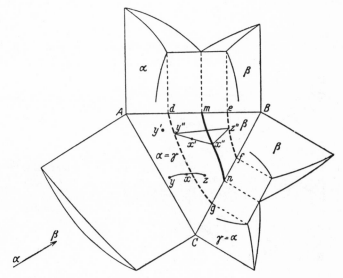

Fig. 49. Triangle of concentrations in the case of two eutectic solubility gaps in the solid state.

at a constant temperature, a condition which would be in contradiction to the phase rule. Furthermore, the untenability of such a construction can be demonstrated on the basis of the group of general laws presented in the appendix to Chapter II.

We shall now take up the consideration of the various state spaces which are developed during the solidification process. Adjoining the homogeneous space of the melt are the two regions of primary crystallization, one of α substance and one of β crystals. The latter are bounded in part by the two homogeneous spaces of α and β substances, respectively, and in the central part of the system by the tubular three-phase space of binary crystallization which has been described. Below the tube is the two-phase space of the mutually saturated solid solutions

α and β. This space is bounded along its two lower sides by the two homogeneous regions of α and β solid solutions.

Let us next consider what form the state space of the β solid solution must have. The discussion of the concentration triangle (Fig. 49) has already demonstrated that for temperatures at which the binary eutectic crystallization occurs along the curve ef, this state space must extend into the interior as far as this curve. Obviously, the boundary which separates it from the space of primary crystallization of β at high temperature is the surface $EBFE$ (Fig. 50). Below the curve EF the state space of β substance is no longer bounded by the region of primary crystallization but by the two-phase region of α and β solid solutions. For this reason the boundary surface of the region of β solid solution must undergo a discontinuous change of direction at the curve EF. The form of the state space of the β solid solution, when viewed in the direction of the arrow $\alpha\beta$ (Fig. 49), is represented schematically in Fig. 53.

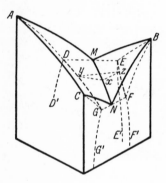

Fig. 50.

Schematic space diagram in the case of two eutectic solubility gaps in the solid state.

The lettering on this figure is the same as on Fig. 50. The two-phase regions which adjoin this single-phase region are indicated on its boundary surfaces. The state space under consideration is bounded on the top by the slanting surface EBF, and on the side toward the region of the $\alpha+\beta$ mixture by the concave surface $E'EFF'$. On the surface EBF, the β solid solution may be said to be saturated with the melt, and, in the same way, on the boundary surface $EFF''E'$ it may be considered to be saturated with α phase.

The region of homogeneous α solid solution differs from that of β in not being located in a corner but along an entire side of the concentration triangle. It is schematically represented in Fig. 54 where it is viewed in the direction reverse to that from which Fig. 53 is seen—that is, as it appears from the corner B. Again the lettering is the same as in the space diagram shown in Fig. 50. The perpendicular planes $CGG'C'$ and $DAA'D'$ are parts of the planes of the two binary systems CB and

AB. Along the surface *CADG* the solid solution, α, is in equilibrium with the melt. Hence, this surface is the boundary between the single-phase region of α solid solution and the two-phase region in which this substance originates. Along the surface *G'GDD'* equilibrium with the β solid solution exists. The surface which bounds the α space must therefore undergo a discontinuous change of direction at the line *GD*.

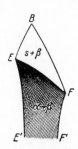

Fig. 53. The space of β solid solution as seen in the direction $\alpha\beta$ (Fig. 49).

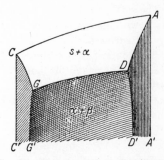

Fig. 54. The space of α solid solution when viewed in the direction opposite to that of Fig. 53.

The surfaces *EBF* and *CGDA* of Figs. 53 and 54 are the solidus surfaces of primary crystallization of β and α solid solutions, respectively.

The regions of primary crystallization of α and β solid solutions are limited above by the liquidus surfaces *AMNC* and *MBN*, respectively (Fig. 50), and below by the solidus surfaces comprising *ADGC* and *EBF*, together with the upper surface of the three-cornered tube of binary eutectic crystallization (Fig. 52). That part of the surface of the three-

Fig. 55.

The space of primary crystallization of β solid solution (Fig. 49).

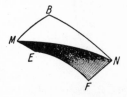

cornered tube designated as *DMNG* forms part of the boundary for the space of the primary crystallization of α, while the surface *EMNF* is similarly related to the primary crystallization of β. The two surfaces intersect along the rib *MN*.

The region of primary crystallization of β, when viewed in the direction of the arrow (Fig. 49) and from somewhat below, has the form given in Fig. 55, in which the lettering corresponds again to that of Fig. 50. *MBN* is the liquidus surface and *MNFE* is the screw-type surface of separation between this region and the three-cornered tube of binary eutectic crystallization. Solidus surface *EBF*, which separates this space from that of the homogeneous β solid solution, is on the back side in Fig. 55. The curves *MB* and *BN* lie in the binary systems *AB* and *BC*.

The space of primary crystallization of α has a form similar to the one just described, but differs from it in having its back portion made up of the side AC instead of being located in a corner.

The state space of the mixture of α and β has the form of a four-edged prism with curved bounding surfaces. On its sides this prism is bounded by the surfaces *G'GDD'* (Fig. 54) and *E'EFF'* (Fig. 53) and by the vertical outer prism surfaces. At the top it is bounded by the interface against the region of binary eutectic crystallization—that is, by the surface which is hidden in Fig. 52. This surface is generated by the motion of the horizontal isothermal line whose ends move along the curves *DG* and *EF*.

In order to obtain a more complete picture of the equilibrium which occurs in the system, we may next consider some horizontal and vertical sections of the space diagram.

2. Isothermal Sections

At a temperature which lies below the melting points of *A* and *B* but is still higher than the melting point of *C* and also higher than the binary eutectic point *M* (Fig. 50), the isothermal section has the form shown in Fig. 56. The largest area represents the still liquid alloys. The

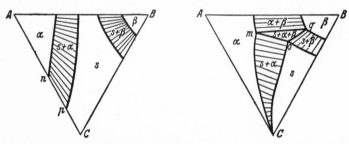

Figs. 56 and 57. Isothermal sections in the case of two eutectic solubility gaps in the solid state.

regions marked α and β represent sections through the spaces of the corresponding homogeneous solid solutions. Fields *s*+α and *s*+β, in which conodes have been drawn, constitute the portions of the isothermal plane which intersect the spaces of primary crystallization.

At the temperature at which *C* melts, which is also above the point *N* (Fig. 50) but below *M*, the isothermal plane cuts through the three curves *MN*, *DG*, and *EF*, corresponding respectively to doubly saturated melt, α solid solution, and β solid solution, in the three points x, y, and z, and hence forms a triangular section of the three-cornered space of binary crystallization, as shown schematically in Fig. 50. This isothermal cut is represented in Fig. 57. The three-phase region xyz is here indicated by the letters omq. Adjacent to this triangle are three two-phase regions —namely, the region $\alpha+\beta$ of the mixture of two solid solutions in which the process of solidification has already been completed, and the regions $s+\alpha$ and $s+\beta$, corresponding to the equilibrium of the melt with α and β solid solutions. Outside these binary regions there are the homogeneous areas s, α, and β.

The position, as shown in Fig. 57, of the two bounding curves mC and oC of the space of the two-phase mixture of melt s and solid solution α is peculiar to the temperature of the melting point of C. This peculiarity is that in their excursion along the sides of the triangle, at only this

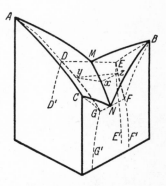

Fɪɢ. 50.

Schematic space diagram in the case of two eutectic solubility gaps in the solid state.

one temperature do the ends of these curves make contact. For all other temperatures, even in the neighborhood of C, they are separate from each other. Above the point C the terminals of these curves lie in the two points n and p, as shown in Fig. 56 where the two-phase system $s+\alpha$ lies entirely to the left of C; for temperatures which are lower, but still above the eutectic point N (Fig. 50), the isothermal section has the form shown in Fig. 58 in which the two points n and p are located to the right of C. This case requires no further discussion. It is readily seen how crystallization has proceeded beyond the stage illustrated in Fig. 57 by extension of the state fields of α, β, and $\alpha+\beta$.

Inspection of Figs. 57 and 58 reveals that the boundary curves of the homogeneous regions α, β, and s have kinks which do not appear in Fig. 56. This situation arises from the fact that in Figs. 57 and 58 the homogeneous phases are in equilibrium with different crystals in different parts of the isothermal section. The discontinuities occur where the plane intersects the various space curves—for example, q (Fig. 57) is

the intersection point of the plane with the curve EF (Fig. 53); m is
the intersection with DG (Fig. 54); and o, with MN (Fig. 50).

As the temperature sinks, the triangle mqo, which is the cross-section
of the three-cornered tube of binary eutectic crystallization, approaches
the side BC and shrinks together. Upon nearing the side BC, the points
m, q, and o all move toward positions on a straight line parallel to the
side BC and eventually coincide with it. When the triangle has shrunk
to a horizontal line lying in the side BC, freezing is complete and the
whole concentration triangle consists of the two single-phase spaces of
α and β solid solutions and the intermediate two-phase region composed
of the mixture of both. The bounding curves in the isothermal plane no
longer show discontinuities since the temperature now being considered
lies underneath the points F of Fig. 53 and G of Fig. 54.

The discussion of the sections shown in Figs. 56-58 makes appropriate
the following remarks confirming the explanations given in the supple-

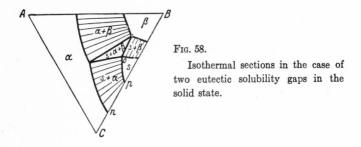

Fig. 58.

Isothermal sections in the case of
two eutectic solubility gaps in the
solid state.

ment to Chapter II. It was there shown that adjoining state spaces
must differ except for some points of contact by exactly one phase, and
that this phase will be present in one of the state spaces but not in the
other. In the present case the homogeneous regions α, β, and s are
bounded by the two-phase spaces $\alpha+\beta$, $s+\alpha$, and $s+\beta$, and these in
turn border the three-phase space $s+\alpha+\beta$. A movement from one single-
phase space into another single-phase space cannot be made directly, but
only by going through a two-phase space. Movement between two two-
phase regions may take place either through a one-phase or through a
three-phase region. For example, in going from $s+\alpha$ to $s+\beta$ (Fig. 57),
the route may pass either through the region of the melt or through the
region of binary eutectic crystallization $s+\alpha+\beta$.

3. Sections Perpendicular to the Plane of Concentration

There remains to be considered the form of the vertical sections. For
purposes of discussion it will be convenient to select the cuts Bm', mn,
and Cp (Fig. 59).

It is readily evident from Fig. 59 that the line formed by the inter-section of the cut Bm' and the surface of the beginning of primary solidification is composed of two segments which meet at the point k lying on the curve of doubly saturated melt. Whether the curve km' climbs in going from k to m' depends upon the form of the space diagram (Fig. 50)—that is, upon how rapidly the temperature of the beginning of freezing falls in going from A to C. If the decrease is very rapid the point m' (Fig. 59) may be at a lower temperature than the point k. In Fig. 60 the opposite situation has been assumed.

For all alloys of the interval kB, the primary precipitation of β sub-stance sets in first. The two-phase region $s+\beta$ lies just below kB' (Fig. 60). Alloys of the part lB complete their solidification in this field and the end product is the homogeneous solid solution β. Thus,

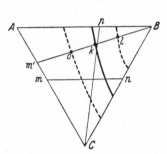

FIG. 59. Position of cuts $m'B$, mn, and Cp.

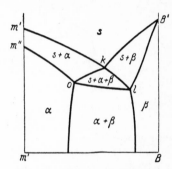

FIG. 60. Section $m'B$ (Fig. 59).

the region $s+\beta$ is bounded by the β area which extends to l (Fig. 59). To the left of l the binary eutectic crystallization of α and β simultaneously, follows upon the conclusion of the primary crystallization of β. In a similar way, solidification of alloys along $m'k$ results in the precipita-tion of primary α solid solution. In the interval $m'o$, α substance is the final product of the freezing process, but along ok a period of binary eutectic crystallization sets in after the primary crystallization has been completed. Since the alloy corresponding to point m' is not a pure component, it does not solidify completely at one temperature, as does the substance B, but freezes during an interval. For this reason the two curves km' and om'' do not intersect at the left side of the diagram in the same way that the curves kB' and lB' do at the right. The region of binary eutectic crystallization is bounded below by an area which repre-sents a mixture of the two solid solutions α and β.

From the discussion concerning the relative positions of the cor-responding points on the three curves mn, ef, and dg (Figs. 49 and 50) it is clear that the triangle okl must be so situated that the line ol uniting the two saturated crystals o and l (which are not in equilibrium with each other since the conodes, in general, lie outside of the plane of this section) is underneath the point k.

The left side of the cut mn (Fig. 61) is quite similar to that of Bm' in appearance. The right side, however, differs from Fig. 60 in that the heterogeneous field $\alpha + \beta$ extends over to the right-hand side, as does likewise the region of binary eutectic crystallization $s + \alpha + \beta$. The two curves kl and ol must intersect each other at l on the right-hand ordinate,

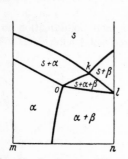

FIG. 61. Section mn (Fig. 59).

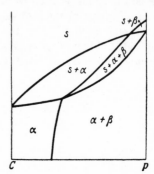

FIG. 62. Section Cp (Fig. 59).

since on the side CB the tube of the binary eutectic solidification degenerates to a horizontal line.

In Fig. 62 is shown the section Cp (Fig. 59) which passes through the corner C. In the segment Ck, α solid solution is precipitated primarily, whereas in the part kp the β solid solution comes out first. For the most part the diagram is exactly similar in form to the cut shown in Fig. 61; but there is one difference, namely, that on account of the low temperature of the point C relative to A and B, all the curves rise in going away from C.

B. PERITECTIC CASE

1. Process of Crystallization. State Spaces

Fig. 63, which illustrates the peritectic case, presents also the second simple example of limited solubility in the solid state. This figure shows a concentration triangle involving two binary peritectic systems with limited solubility. Certain features which occur during the process of solidification of such a system are quite similar to those in the ternary system just described. Only two types of solid substances appear, both of which extend across the concentration diagram from one binary system to another. Their boundaries, at the finish of solidification, are indicated by the curves dg and ef. Furthermore, the curve of doubly saturated melt must connect the two peritectic points m and n, because in the absence of a third solid phase, solidification comes to an end without encountering a ternary eutectic or peritectic point. The next problem for consideration concerns the manner in which the process of solidification is changed from that in Section A by the peritectic arrangement of curves *mn*, *dg*, and *ef*. The ternary space diagram of the peritectic case is presented in Fig. 64, in which the capital letters correspond to the small letters of Fig. 63. The solidification of all alloys of the concentration region *MBN* begins with the precipitation of the homogeneous β solid solution. The state space *E'EBFF'* of this phase has the same general form as the corresponding space shown in Fig. 53 for the system

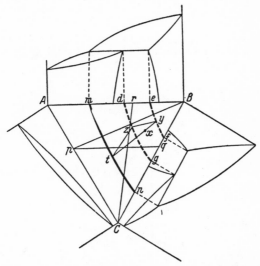

Fig. 63. Triangle of concentrations in the case of two peritectic solubility gaps in the solid state.

with a eutectic solubility gap. Solidification at first proceeds exactly as for homogeneous solid solutions. If the alloy lies within the region of homogeneous β solid solution, the melt will be consumed by the freezing process before it reaches the limit of saturation with respect to the β phase. During freezing of alloys in the region *mefn*, the composition of the β substance reaches the boundary curve *ef*—for example, for an alloy *x* at some point *y* (Fig. 64)—while simultaneously the concentration of the melt arrives at point *t* on the curve *mn*. The melt *t* and the solid solution *y* are now in equilibrium with the α solid solution at the point *z* —that is, both are saturated with α crystals, a condition which means that the region of binary peritectic crystallization has been reached. These relations are illustrated on a magnified scale in Fig. 65; *tzy* represents the position of the three-phase triangle at the beginning of the peritectic solidification. As the temperature decreases, the compositions of the three phases are displaced along the curves *DG*, *EF*, and *MN*, (Fig. 64) in the downward direction. Corresponding to the geometric arrangement of Figs. 63 and 64, the direction of displacement is indicated by the arrows yy', zz', and tt'.

It is now appropriate to ask what significance is attached to the term "binary peritectic" in comparison with "binary eutectic" when ternary systems are concerned, and what geometric conditions are connected to binary peritectic processes. At the eutectic point of a binary system the melt *s* breaks up into the two constituents of the eutectic, the crystalline substances α and β: $s \rightarrow \alpha + \beta$. On the other hand, in the peritectic case the melt *s* reacts with one crystalline substance α to form a new substance β: $s + \alpha \rightarrow \beta$. Since both equilibria are invariant, the question as to which of the two processes occurs is answered at once by determining the concentrations of the three participating phases. If the concentration

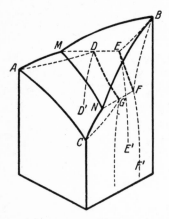

Fig. 64.

Space diagram corresponding to Fig. 63.

of the melt *s* lies between the two solid substances α and β the reaction must be of a eutectic nature. However, if the concentration of one of the two substances—for example, β—is between that of the melt and the other solid solution, the peritectic process is involved. In a ternary system, similar relationships exist, as discussed for invariant equilibrium in the previous chapter. For mono-variant equilibrium, conditions are more complicated because the compositions of all participating phases change during the binary eutectic or peritectic reaction. For example, one phase, as the melt, may be consumed not only by conversion into solid solutions but also by absorption by these solid solutions as they change composition through diffusion. Crystallization may be termed "binary eutectic" when the amount of solid phases increases and the quantity of melt decreases, and called "binary peritectic" if the amount of the melt and of one of the solid phases decreases. Observation of the conode triangle will indicate which process is proceeding.

In the investigation of the movement of this triangle the assumption will be made, for the sake of simplicity, that the three arrows which indicate the direction of the change of concentration of the three phases are parallel to each other and similarly inclined to the axis of temperature. Then during a period of crystallization, the triangle zyt will experience a displacement only, but not a change of form or size. Next, let it be assumed that the points z, y, and t are displaced during crystallization in the directions zz', yy', tt' toward z', y', and t', respectively. Further, let x' be the composition of the alloy. Before the displacement, the ratio of the amount of phase y to the total amount of alloy x' is given by the ratio of the length ux' to the total length uy (see Chapter I, section 2). After the displacement of the concentrations into the new

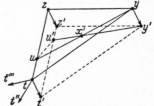

Fig. 65.

Changes in concentration for binary eutectic and peritectic reactions.

positions y', z', and t', this ratio becomes $u'x'/u'y'$. Inspection shows that the amount of y has decreased. The necessary condition that the ratio should not change—that is, the proportion of y should not be altered —is that the segments yy' and $u'u$ remain parallel to each other. In other words, the displacement yy' must take place in the direction of the side zt of the triangle. If the direction of the displacement corresponds to the arrow tt'', the amount of y increases. A similar analysis makes evident the fact that the percentage of solid, z, increases in either case.

It is possible to deduce from the position of the path of crystallization what kind of process is taking place in the three-phase space. If the arrow which indicates the change of concentration of the melt points away from the triangle as tt'' (Fig. 65), a eutectic crystallization is in progress.* If it has the direction tt', there occurs instead a peritectic

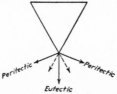

* Note by translator: By "away from the triangle," Masing apparently means in a direction lying between the extended sides as in the figure. If the displacement is to either side of this vertical angle, the reaction is of the peritectic type.

reaction, $y+t \rightarrow z$, in which both y and t are consumed but t is used up first. In case the displacement is in the direction tt''', the phase z is consumed; whereas the amount of y increases. On the other hand, as mentioned above, if the arrow points in the direction zt, the quantity of the phase y will remain unchanged and the process will consist simply in the precipitation of solid solution z from melt t. Displacement in the direction yt leaves the quantity of z unchanged. These last cases occur only rarely and will therefore be passed over without further comment.

The above discussion shows that, unlike a binary system, a ternary one permits continuous transformation from the eutectic to the peritectic type of reaction corresponding to a shift of the direction of the arrow which indicates the change of concentration of the phases.

After this introduction, no difficulty should be experienced in securing a general view of the complete system. The surface of the beginning of crystallization consists, as is evident from Fig. 64, of two sheets which intersect along the curve MN of doubly saturated melt. On the sheet $AMNC$ the crystallization of α begins, while on the sheet MBN, β solid solution appears. The melts whose compositions lie on the line MN are saturated in both α and β. Freezing of such alloys begins at once with the binary peritectic solidification.

The region of primary crystallization is bounded above by the surface which marks the beginning of freezing. Its remaining boundaries are formed by the sides of the prism, the surfaces of the end of solidification of solid solution β (EBF) and solid solution α ($ADGC$), and the surfaces by which it is separated from the space of binary peritectic crystallization. That part of the last-named region which is connected with the primary solidification of β is the surface which is formed by the gliding of a horizontal line from me through the position ty to nf (Fig. 63). Similarly, for the crystallization of α it is the surface generated by the movement of a line from md through zt to ng. The line zy, which generates the third boundary of the three-cornered tube of binary peritectic freezing, is not concerned with the region of primary crystallization, since its movement forms the under boundary of the three-phase space against the two-phase space occupied by the mixture of solid solutions α and β.

The space of primary crystallization of β has exactly the same form as described for the eutectic case of Fig. 55. The region of primary crystallization of α solid solution in the peritectic system differs from the corresponding space in the eutectic case only in having its edge AC (Fig. 64) below MN. As a consequence, the surface $MDGN$ separating this space from the region of binary peritectic solidification constitutes its upper boundary instead of a lower, as in the eutectic system.

The state space of homogeneous β solid solution has already been described. The space of the homogeneous α solid solution resembles the corresponding region in the eutectic system (Fig. 54), except that the edge *DG* lies at a higher temperature than *AC*.

The region of binary peritectic crystallization is a three-cornered tube similar to that previously described (see Fig. 52), the difference being that the isothermal triangle which moves along the curves *EF*, *DG*, and *MN* to form the three-cornered tube has what may be called its "liquidus corner" following along *MN* (Fig. 64), or *mn* (Fig. 63), at one side of the curves *dg* and *ef*. On the sides of the prism corresponding to the binary systems *AB* and *BC* this peritectic tube degenerates to a single isothermal line.

The region of the mixture of the two solid solutions α and β has the form of an upright curved prism. Above, it is limited by the surface developed by the gliding of the horizontal line from *DE* to *FG*, on two sides by the bounding planes of the state prism, and on the other two by the surface *E'EFF'* (Fig. 64) which separates it from the β solid solution and a similar boundary against the α solid solution.

Summarizing, the entire system consists of three homogeneous regions, one of melt and the two solid solutions α and β; of two spaces of primary crystallization; one of binary peritectic crystallization; and the region of the binary mixture of the solid solutions α and β. This general description can be understood better by consideration of isothermal and vertical sections such as have been used in discussing previous structures.

2. Isothermal Sections. Sections Perpendicular to the Plane of Concentration

At a temperature below the melting point of *B* but above that of *M* and *N* (Fig. 64) the crystallization of β material will have started (Fig. 66), but the largest part of the system will still be liquid. The two homogeneous regions of melt *s* and solid solution β are separated by the band *s* + β.

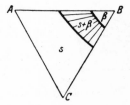

Fig. 66.

Isothermal sections in the case of two peritectic gaps in the solid state.

At temperatures below *M* but still above *N* the situation depicted in Fig. 67 exists. Since binary peritectic crystallization is in progress, the isothermal cut will contain the three-phase conode triangle *tzy*. The corners of this triangle touch the homogeneous regions and therefore designate the compositions of the three homogeneous phases which are in equilibrium with each other at the given temperature. Since the

solidification of α substance has begun, there will be a region of homogeneous α solid solution. The significance of the several fields agrees with
the corresponding fields shown in Fig. 58 except for characteristic differences required by the form of the diagram—for example, the region of
the melt which still remains lies on the side *AC*. This character of the

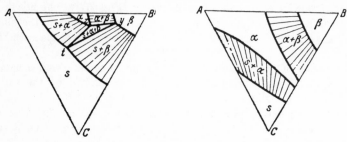

FIGS. 67 and 68. Isothermal sections in the case of two peritectic gaps in the solid
state.

section is maintained until the temperature drops to *N* (Fig. 64). Then,
the triangle *yzt* approaches the side *BC* of the concentration triangle
(Fig. 67), until finally all three points, *y*, *z*, and *t* make contact simultaneously.

At a temperature below *N* and *A* the horizontal section has the form
shown in Fig. 68. The field of α solid solution now extends through to

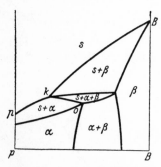

FIG. 69. Section *pB* (Fig. 63).

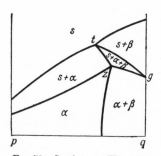

FIG. 70. Section *pq* (Fig. 63).

the side *BC*; hence, the molten substance can no longer exist in equilibrium with β but only with α solid solution.

Finally, let us consider the three vertical cuts *Bp*, *pq*, and *Cr* (Fig. 63).
The first of these is exhibited in Fig. 69. It has a form quite analogous
to the section given in Fig. 60, but because of the peritectic character
of the ternary space diagram and the consequent difference in the liquidus

surface, certain variations occur. The point k, which represents the doubly saturated melt, lies to the left of the solid solution o instead of being at the right, as in Fig. 60.

The cut pq is shown in Fig. 70. This figure is analogous to Fig. 61 and requires, therefore, no complete discussion. The three-phase field $s+\alpha+\beta$ falls away on the right to g, as shown in the figure, for reasons which will be obvious from a comparison of the relative positions of the cut pq and the triangle yzt (Fig. 63). It will be seen that this triangle, as it is displaced toward the side BC with decreasing temperature, will first touch the section pq with the corner t. For this reason, point t in Fig. 70 will lie at the highest temperature. The point z of this triangle

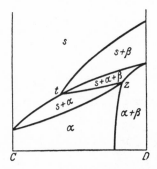

Fig. 71.

Section Cr (Fig. 63).

will next reach the section and will have the second highest temperature. The third corner, y, of the three-phase space, as shown in Fig. 70, lies at the lowest temperature of the three points. The cut Cr has the form shown in Fig. 71, which may be compared with Fig. 62. The point t must lie lower than z for, as seen from Figs. 63 and 67, the latter reaches the vertical section at a higher temperature than the former. For the rest, the cut Cr may be visualized without additional discussion.

C. Transformation of a Eutectic into a Peritectic System

If the solubility gap in the one binary system has a peritectic character while that in the other is a eutectic type, there must take place within the ternary system a transformation of the one type into the other. It has already been pointed out that the binary peritectic can pass into the binary eutectic by a continuous change in the form of the conode triangle of the three-phase space.

Fig. 72 represents the triangle of concentrations for this structural case. Since, as in the systems just described, the present diagram is concerned with only two different crystal forms, the process of solidification proceeds without the appearance of a four-phase invariant equilibrium.

The concentration point, m, representing the melt in the binary system AB, must lie to the left of d, whereas the corresponding composition, n, in the system BC is located to the right of g. It is evident that the two curves dg and mn must cross somewhere inside the ternary system. The conode triangles yzt, $y'z't'$, and $y''z''t''$ indicate how this transformation from a peritectic configuration to a eutectic arrangement takes place within the ternary system. The crossing point of the two curves mn and dg has no real significance, as consideration of the triangle $y'z't'$ will show immediately. All points of this triangle lie at the same temperature.

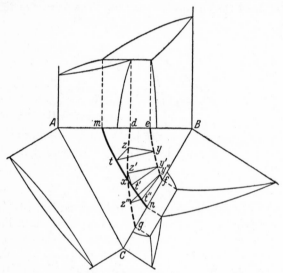

Fig. 72. Triangle of concentrations in the case of one peritectic and one eutectic solubility gap in the solid state in the binary systems.

From the nature of the binary diagrams which form the sides AB and BC, the curves mn, dg, and ef must fall continuously in going from the side AB to the side BC. Hence, the point t' on the curve mn lies at a lower temperature than the point x on the same curve. On the other hand, on the curve dg the point z' lies at a higher temperature than the point x. Hence, intersection does not actually occur, but the curve mn of the doubly saturated melt passes above the curve dg of saturated solid solution at x.

The space figure of the constitutional case being considered will be found in Fig. 73 in which, as is usually the case, the capital letters correspond to the lower case type in Fig. 72. There is now no difficulty in obtaining a comprehensive view of the process of solidification and of the several state spaces and state surfaces which exist. The relations correspond completely to those given for the two structural cases which have just been described. The three-edged region of binary peritectic and eutectic solidification is of some interest. It is shown schematically in Fig. 74 in a perspective view as seen when observed in the direction from C toward AB. Near the side AB the rib MN hides the rib DG; the latter comes into view at R near the middle of the ternary system and continues to be visible. The curve MN turns sharply to the right as

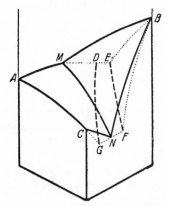

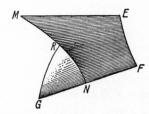

FIG. 73. Space diagram corresponding to Fig. 72.

FIG. 74. Three-phase space for the freezing porcess illustrated in Figs. 72 and 73.

it approaches N. This reversal of the relative positions of the two curves is characteristic of the passage from a peritectic to a eutectic system.

Since the present case offers nothing essentially new over those which have just been discussed, consideration of isothermal and vertical sections will be omitted. For a vertical section parallel to the side AB and moving away from it there occurs a transformation from the type of diagram shown in Fig. 70 to that given in Fig. 61.

Chapter VI

All Three Binary Systems Without Compounds but Having Solid Solutions with Solubility Gaps in the Solid State

1. Process of Crystallization

We turn now to the consideration of a case which may be viewed as a more general form of the problem of mechanical mixtures treated in Chapter II—that is, a ternary system for which all three binary systems exhibit eutectics and possess limited solid solubility. If we assume certain limiting conditions—namely, that the solid solubility gap does not vanish within the ternary system (such a disappearance is possible and will be encountered later in Chapter VIII) and that no new types of crystals appear—certain statements concerning the constitution of the alloys in

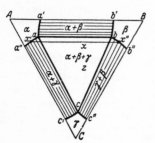

Fig. 75.

Isothermal section after conclusion of freezing in the case of solubility gaps in all three binary systems.

the solid state may be made immediately. At each corner there will be a region of homogeneous solid solution. Each such region will be bounded by surfaces over which the first solid solution is saturated with solid solutions existing at the other two corners. For example, over a portion of its bounding surface the A-rich α solid solution will be saturated with the B-rich β crystals, and over another portion with the C-rich γ crystals. Consider an isothermal section through the system in the solid state. The intersection of this plane with the bounding surfaces just mentioned will form bounding curves, which for the α solid solution will have the segments $a''a$ and aa', as shown in Fig. 75. The discontinuity at a arises because along the segment $a'a$, the solid solution α is in equilibrium with and saturated with β phase, and along aa'', with γ substance. At a, it is saturated with both β and γ phases, and hence is in equilibrium with both types of crystals. The fields of homogeneous γ and β solid solutions will exhibit very similar boundaries, as has been illustrated in the figure.

The α solid solution on the curve $a'a$ is in equilibrium with β solid solution of varying composition indicated by the points on the curve $b'b$ and, mutually, the β solid solution is in equilibrium with α phase of variable composition. The alloys of intermediate concentration—that is, those in the region $a'b'ba$, where ab is a straight line—consist of mixtures of α and β solid solutions. The system of conodes indicates how the various alloys in this two-phase region are composed of two mutually saturated solid solutions in equilibrium with each other. In the same way, the alloys of the region $a''acc'$ are composed of crystals of α and γ and the alloys of the region $c''b''bc$ of γ and β.

Next consider the alloys inside the triangle abc. These are composed of three kinds of solid solutions whose respective compositions correspond to the points a, b, and c. This fact may be demonstrated by the following analysis. Let a point x within the triangle be selected, and let it be assumed that a straight line drawn through it, as shown in the figure, encounters the curve aa'' of α solution saturated with γ at x' and the curve bb'' of β solid solution saturated with γ at x''. Furthermore, as an experiment, let it be assumed that the alloy x is composed of the two crystalline types x' and x''. Both, however, are saturated with γ, and hence are in equilibrium with γ. Therefore this arrangement is fundamentally equivalent to equilibrium among the three phases α, β, and γ. If the pressure and the temperature in such a system are held constant there can be no degrees of freedom—that is, the composition of the different phases cannot change when the composition of x is altered. This result comes about because the original assumption was not justifiable.* Therefore, an alloy x cannot be composed of solid solutions x' and x'', but it—and all alloys within the triangle abc—must be composed of the three phases with compositions a, b, and c. The triangle abc is a three-phase region in the solid state.

The solid alloys may be divided into three groups according to the nature of the phase spaces in which they lie. These are: (1) the homogeneous α, β, and γ solid solution regions, (2) the three regions of two-phase alloys consisting respectively of $\alpha+\beta$, $\alpha+\gamma$, and $\beta+\gamma$ solid solutions, and (3) the region of three-phase alloys of which the structural constituents are the three crystalline types α, β, and γ—that is, the alloys inside of the triangle abc.

---

* Note by translator: The hypothesis is impossible at the start. The α solid solution is assumed to be in equilibrium with γ phase of one composition and the β solid solution in equilibrium with γ phase of a different composition, but the definition of a phase is a portion of matter which is homogeneous in composition, etc. Hence the original assumption leads to an impossible situation and cannot be correct.

Comparison of the relations existing in this system with those in the simple mechanical mixture described in Chapter II shows at once how much more complicated the diagram has become through the formation of solid solutions in the corners of the triangle. In the former case there was in the solid state only the one field involving the mixture of the three pure components; here there are no less than seven different state regions. It appears also that the space diagram for a simple mechanical mixture is a special case of the system under discussion and may be assumed to originate when the homogeneous regions of α, β, and γ solid

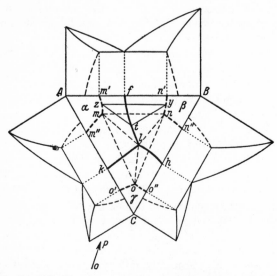

Fɪɢ. 76. Triangle of concentrations in the case of eutectic solubility gaps in all three binary systems.

solutions shrink down to the pure components and the corresponding binary state fields $\alpha+\beta$, $\beta+\gamma$, and $\alpha+\gamma$ vanish into the binary systems AB, BC, and AC.

In Fig. 76 the concentration triangle is exhibited in the usual manner. In order to avoid any possibility of confusion of the two types of diagrams, the distinction between this diagram and the one shown in Fig. 75 will be emphasized (also refer to Chapter II). The latter represents an isothermal cut through the space diagram of the alloy system. It indicates, by the use of conodes, the various phases which are in equilibrium with each other along the boundary lines. On the other hand, Fig. 76 shows the projection of the space diagram on the plane of concentrations. The bounding lines of the state surfaces which are given therein do not correspond to a fixed temperature. This figure is well adapted to provide a comprehensive view of the whole solidification process, but does not specify what phases are in equilibrium with each other.

The lines of intersection of the bounding surfaces of the liquid state are drawn solid in Fig. 76. The heavy dotted lines mark the intersections of the surfaces which bound the homogeneous solid solution regions. It has been assumed that changes of the saturation boundaries of the solid solution with decreasing temperature may be neglected.

The following remarks may be made concerning the form of the liquidus surface. Corresponding to the three kinds of solid solution which are precipitated out, there exist three continuous curved sheets, each of which specifies the temperature and composition of melt saturated with one of the three solid phases. These portions intersect in curves fl, hl, and kl along which the melt is simultaneously saturated in two kinds of solid solution. The common intersection point l of the three curves corresponds to a liquid composition which is simultaneously saturated in the three crystalline forms α, β, and γ. Hence, for constant pressure this point represents an invariant, four-phase equilibrium. Therefore, l must be either a ternary eutectic or a ternary peritectic point. For a simple mixture without the formation of solid solution the latter possibility does not exist. In the present instance it may occur under certain conditions concerning which we shall shortly have something to say. Fig. 76 evidently represents the eutectic arrangement because the point l lies within the triangle mno formed by the three crystalline phases which are in equilibrium. (More will be said about this triangle later.) Obviously, solidification must be complete at the point l, from which fact one deduces that the curves fl, hl, and kl, which start out from the points f, h, and k, respectively, and extend into the interior of the triangle, must descend to lower temperatures, and that l must lie at the lowest temperature. It is also clear that the points m, n, o, and l, lie at the same temperature—that of the ternary eutectic point. As an illustration of the liquidus surface, which has just been described, the same diagram will serve as was shown in Fig. 9 (p. 16) for the case of a simple mechanical mixture without the formation of solid solution.

The solidification of alloys which in the solid state have either single-phase or two-phase structures follows in exactly the same way as was described in Chapter V. During the process of solidification the state point of the melt moves along the liquidus while the corresponding state point of the precipitated solid moves along over the solidus surface. If the composition of the alloy lies within one of the homogeneous regions of solid solution α, β, or γ, the molten material will all be used, and the solidification process finished before the path of the melt meets one of the curves of binary eutectic crystallization fl, hl, or kl—that is, before a second type of solid begins to be precipitated (Fig. 76). If the alloy has two phases in the solid state, then after the termination of the process of primary crystallization of one solid form—for example, β, which is indicated by the melt reaching either fl or hl—the binary eutectic solidification begins. These binary eutectic processes occur in exactly the same way as has been described in Chapter V. They are completed when the conode joining the two solid solutions in equilibrium with each other moves into such a position that it includes the point representing the composition of the alloy. This geometric situation signifies that the molten material has been consumed and the solidification process finished. Obviously, this analysis applies only to those alloys which lie within one of the binary portions $aa'b'b$, $bb''c''c$, or $acc'a''$ (Fig. 75). For alloys within the triangle abc, the liquid substance becomes saturated in the third crystalline constituent before the conode which combines the first two solid forms to be precipitated has moved into a position to include the point which represents the composition of the alloy. For all alloys, ternary eutectic crystallization at the invariant equilibrium point must take place at the end of the binary solidification period. In this region the space of binary eutectic crystallization is bounded below by the horizontal plane passing through the ternary eutectic point.

If the changes of concentration of the solid solutions are disregarded, the points a, b, and c and so forth of Fig. 75 correspond to the points m, n, and o and so forth of Fig. 76. The constitutional case being analyzed offers the opportunity of extending the discussion of binary and ternary eutectic crystallization processes beyond the limits reached in Chapter II. During binary eutectic crystallization only one degree of freedom exists, and this statement is valid for each of the three participating phases. Hence, there corresponds to each of the phases, not a surface but only a curve in the space diagram. For the doubly saturated melt this curve is the intersection of two sheets of the surface of primary crystallization—e.g., one of the curves fl, hl, or kl (Fig. 76). In a similar manner, corresponding curves which specify the composition of the doubly saturated solid solutions existing in equilibrium with the melt may also be represented as the intersection of two simply saturated surfaces. For example, the curve $n'n$ indicates that the β solid solution, which participates in the binary eutectic solidification, is simultaneously in equilibrium with melt and α solid solution. This curve is the intersection of two surfaces which constitute two portions of the boundary of the space of β solid solution. The first is the surface over which the β phase is saturated with melt—that is, the solidus surface of the primary solidification of β substance whose projection is represented in Fig. 76 by the surface $Bn'nn''$. The second is the surface over which the β phase is saturated with α. For the sake of simplicity the latter surface has been assumed to extend vertically downward so that its projection upon the horizontal plane may be represented by $n'n$. The curve $n'n$ is therefore the intersection of two bounding surfaces of a phase space in the same way as has been specified for the curve fl. The fact that in Chapter II curves of the type represented by fl appeared to be of a special type arose from the circumstance that when no solid solution is formed the space of homogeneous solid solution degenerates to a vertical line coincident with the concentration of the pure component. These ideas could have been applied in Chapter V in the discussion of the eutectic and peritectic cases.

Naturally, similar considerations apply to both the other cases of binary eutectic crystallization which occur in this diagram. There is general validity to the law which states that corresponding to a three-phase equilibrium there are three curves, each of which lies in the bounding surface of one of the participating phases and represents a discontinuity on this bounding surface such that upon passing across it the second phase, in which the originally considered phase is saturated, is a different one.

The three-phase space originates then by the movement of horizontal conodes between each pair of the three curves mentioned in the previous paragraph. It starts out from the eutectic line in the binary system, expands to a three-cornered tube in the interior of the space diagram, and in the present instance, is bounded below by the horizontal plane of the ternary eutectic. It is, in fact, brought abruptly to an end by this plane which corresponds to the saturation of the melt in three different kinds of crystalline substances, and therefore indicates a four-phase equilibrium. Each of the three spaces of binary eutectic crystallization resembles the form illustrated in Fig. 12, except that in the present instance the back side does not coincide with a binary system but extends inside the state prism. Actually, the rear portion of the tube is generated by the gliding of a conode—for example, the line $m'n'$ in Fig. 76 along the curves $m'm$ and $n'n$. The triangle yzt represents an isothermal section through the three-cornered tube of binary eutectic crystallization of α and β. The line yz is not, in general, parallel to the side AB of the concentration triangle, and this statement is also true of mn.

The intersection of the three curves of doubly saturated melt fl, kl, and hl in the ternary eutectic point has been noted. To all these curves one phase—the melt—is common, whereas the solid substances in equilibrium with it are different for each line. In the same way the points m, n, and o (Fig. 76) must each represent intersection points of three curves lying in the boundary surfaces of a homogeneous region. It is obvious at once that such is the case. Let us consider, for example, the point n. At this point the β solid solution is in equilibrium with the melt and the two saturated crystalline substances α and γ. Summation of the combinations of three phases which include β as a participant yields the three groups $\beta+\alpha+s$, $\beta+\gamma+s$, and $\beta+\gamma+\alpha$. The first two correspond to the previously mentioned ribs on the surface of the space of homogeneous β substance. They arise from the binary eutectic crystallization of $\beta+\alpha$ in the one case and $\beta+\gamma$ in the other. The third corresponds to a rib produced by the junction of the surfaces over which β is saturated with α and with γ, respectively. These surfaces have already been described. For the sake of simplicity, it is assumed that they are vertical —that is, any dependence of the degree of saturation of solid solution upon temperature is neglected. Their intersection will therefore be a straight line perpendicular to the plane of concentration. This line cannot be seen, since in Fig. 76 its projection coincides with the point n. These three curves meeting at point n are equivalent from the standpoint of phase theory. The emphasis which has frequently been placed on the first two is the result of the considerable interest which has been attached to the process of solidification. However, the developments of the last few years have shown that the position of the equilibrium surfaces in the solid state is very influential in relation to the behavior of alloys. Indeed, as a rule it is more important to know the position of the boundary surfaces in the solid state and also their curves of intersection —which, in general, are not straight lines—than it is to have complete knowledge of the process of solidification. In the same way, the points m and o may be shown to be the intersection points of three bounding curves of doubly saturated solid phases.

The above facts have general application. Each of the four points of invariant equilibrium is the intersection of three curves of three-phase equilibrium. Each of the three curves has associated with it one phase which is common to all. This phase is the one whose composition corresponds to the point of invariant equilibrium—for example, for the β phase the point n, for the γ phase the point o, for the α phase the point m, and for the melt s the point l (L).

The light dotted lines mn, no, om, ml, nl, ol have another meaning. They are the ribs on the surfaces of two-phase spaces. Concerning them, more will be said later.

2. State Spaces

The discussion has now progressed to a point which affords a general view of all the state spaces which are developed as the result of solidification. The regions of binary eutectic crystallization have already been discussed in a preliminary way. The regions of homogeneous solid solution have a form like that shown in Fig. 77 in which the space of β solid solution is viewed in the direction from the side AC toward B. The lettering corresponds to that in Fig. 76. $Bn'nn''$ is the surface over which the β solid solution is saturated with the melt—that is, the solidus surface; $n'nn_1n'_1$ is the surface of saturation of β solid solution in the α phase and $n''nn_1n''_1$ is its surface of saturation with γ. In this figure the more general case has been assumed in that the position of these surfaces depends upon the temperature. The region is bounded behind by the planes of the binary systems AB and BC. The ribs $n'n$, nn_1, and nn'' indicate the curves along which the β solid solution is saturated in two other phases and the point n gives the composition of β during the invariant eutectic equilibrium. There are corresponding spaces for the other two solid solution types α and γ.

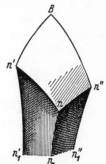

FIG. 77.

The state space of the homogeneous solid solutions α, β, or γ (Fig. 76).

There is a certain similarity between the solid region which has just been described and the corresponding one in Chapter V. The principal difference is that in the present case the curves of doubly saturated crystals do not extend to the sides of the prism but are intersected inside by other similar curves.

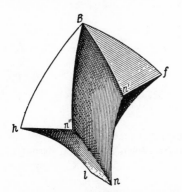

FIG. 78. The state space of primary crystallization (Fig. 76).

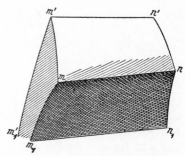

FIG. 79. State space of the mixture of two crystalline types $\alpha + \beta$, $\beta + \gamma$, or $\alpha + \gamma$ (Figs. 75 and 76).

The regions of homogeneous solid solution are bounded above by spaces of primary crystallization—that is, by two-phase spaces containing molten material and one type of crystalline solid. The latter spaces are in turn bounded by liquidus surfaces. The region of primary crystallization of β material is shown schematically in Fig. 78 where the observer is looking from behind B toward the side AC. In this figure the lettering corresponds to that used in Fig. 76. The two sheets hBn'' and fBn' are plane surfaces and lie in the sides of the prism of state. The solidus surface $Bn''nn'$ (Fig. 77), which limits the region of β solid solution, has been exposed by the removal of the space of this substance so that the state space as shown in Fig. 78 has a hollowed-out form; $hn''nl$ and $fn'nl$ are the two surfaces which separate the region under consideration from the two three-phase spaces of binary eutectic crystallization involving β. The upper bounding surface $hBfl$, which is the liquidus surface of the β crystals, is turned away from the observer.

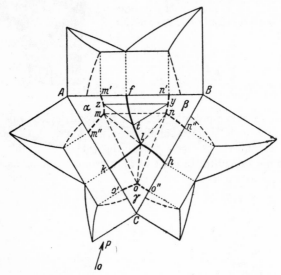

Fig. 76. Triangle of concentrations in the case of eutectic solubility gaps in all three binary systems.

There is a marked similarity between this state space and the corresponding one for the simple mechanical mixture shown in Fig. 11, except for the removal of the region of homogeneous β solid solution. Corresponding spaces of primary crystallization exist for the α and γ forms.

Spaces which include two solid crystalline forms will next be considered. These are the regions $mnn'm'$ (Fig. 76) for the mixture of α and β, $n''o''on$ for β and γ, and $m''o'om$ for the mixture of α and γ solid solutions. The general form of these regions is illustrated by the α and β mixture shown in Fig. 79 in which the observer looks in the direction of the arrow OP (Fig. 76). At the rear, the space is bounded by the perpendicular plane of the binary system AB. The surface $m'mm_1m'_1$ separates it from the region of homogeneous α solid solution, while the face $n'nn_1n'_1$

which is turned away from view is the boundary against the homogeneous β solid solution. In agreement with the assumption that the solubility in the solid state changes with temperature, these two bounding surfaces are both curved; but no statement can be made concerning their exact form. The surface $m'n'nm$ is the boundary against the three-cornered region of binary eutectic solidification of α and β. The face mnn_1m_1 separates the region under consideration from the three-phase space of the mixture of solid α, β, and γ. Since the latter two surfaces of inhomogeneous regions are boundaries that are generated by the movement of conodes along the curves $m'n$ and $n'n$ in the one case and the curves mm_1 and nn_1 in the other, their intersections with the isothermal planes are straight lines. The three-phase space which contains the three solid solutions is outlined by the triangle mno as it slides down to lower temperatures. In general, the positions of its corners will vary with temperature on account of changes in solubility of the homogeneous phases. This region has the form of an approximately vertical, three-cornered tube. Fundamentally, it does not differ particularly from the three-phase space of binary solidification.

The 14 different regions of state may be summarized as follows:

(1) The region of molten substance s,

(2) Three regions of primary solidification of α, β, and γ, respectively,

(3) Three regions of binary eutectic solidification of the combinations $\alpha+\beta$, $\beta+\gamma$, and $\alpha+\gamma$,

(4) Three homogeneous regions of the solid solutions α, β, and γ, respectively,

(5) Three spaces of mixtures of two different solid solutions $\alpha+\beta$, $\alpha+\gamma$, and $\beta+\gamma$,

(6) One three-phase space containing a mixture of the three solid solutions α, β, and γ.

One sees readily how complicated the whole situation is in comparison with the simple mechanical mixture without solid solution which was described in Chapter II. This complication has come about from the presence of a region of homogeneous solid solution about each component.

It has already been mentioned that the straight lines which combine the points m, n, o, and l of the several phases taking part in the invariant eutectic equilibrium correspond to ribs on the bounding surfaces of two-phase spaces. The way in which these ribs originate is obvious. The rib mn, which is shown in Fig. 79, comes at the junction of the two bounding surfaces one of which separates the two-phase space containing α and β solid solutions from the space of binary eutectic crystallization of these two substances, and the other separates it from the region of the mixture of α, β, and γ. The lines no and mo have a corresponding significance for the substances $\beta+\gamma$ and $\alpha+\gamma$. As shown in Fig. 78, the line ln is the isothermal rib at the bottom of the two-phase space of the primary crystallization of β. In a similar manner the rib ml arises from the primary crystallization of α, and rib lo from the primary crystallization of γ.

Finally, if one considers the several triangles which are formed by taking three at a time the four phases participating in the invariant equilibrium—namely, the triangles mln, nlo, mlo, and mno—it will be observed that each of these represents a plane section through a three-phase space, and in fact is the terminal plane of the space. For example, mln is the lower boundary plane of the region of binary eutectic solidification of α and β; nlo has the corresponding significance for β and γ, as does likewise mlo for α and γ. The triangle mno is the upper boundary plane of the region of the three crystalline forms α, β, and γ. The fact that this triangle coincides with the plane of invariant equilibrium has no particular significance, and comes about only because l lies within

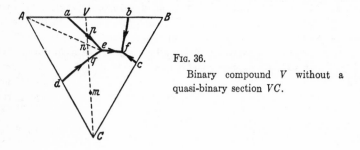

Fig. 36.

Binary compound V without a quasi-binary section VC.

the triangle formed by m, n, and o. In the peritectic case—for example that shown in Chapter IV, Fig. 36—the conditions are otherwise. In the invariant peritectic shown in this figure the four phases in equilibrium are the melt e and the crystalline forms A, C, and V. The aggregate of the contributing phases forms a quadrilateral $AVeC$ instead of corresponding to some triangle. In this system (Chapter IV) there are two regions which lie above the peritectic plane and terminate on it—namely, the space of binary eutectic crystallization of A and V (triangle AVe) and a similar space for A and C (triangle ACe). There are also two regions which begin with triangles lying in the peritectic plane and extend down to lower temperatures. One of these triangles is AVC which is the upper boundary of the region containing solid A, V, and C, and the other is VeC which is the top surface of the space of binary eutectic crystallization of V and C.

A general significance is attached to these relationships. The partial triangles associated with a plane of invariant equilibrium are boundaries of three-phase regions which terminate upon this plane. Further, the lines which connect the various state points of this plane correspond to ribs in the boundary surfaces of adjoining bi-variant two-phase spaces. At the corners, the invariant figures touch the spaces of the homogeneous substances which contribute to the equilibrium. Also, at each corner three curves cross, each of which represents the corresponding temperatures and compositions of one of the phases saturated with the other two. It is helpful to keep these relationships in mind as an aid in making space diagrams and also as a useful check against errors in the completed structures.

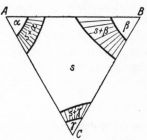

Fɪɢ. 80.

Isothermal section for the structural type shown in Fig. 76 before the beginning of eutectic crystallization.

3. Isothermal Sections

The form of the isothermal sections may be derived from the space diagram already described. When the temperature is still above the highest binary eutectic but below the melting point of all the components, the isothermal section has the form shown in Fig. 80. Besides the homogeneous regions there may be seen the two-phase regions of primary solidification. As soon as the temperature drops below the highest

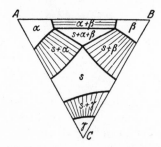

Fɪɢ. 81. Isothermal section after the beginning of eutectic crystallization of α and β.

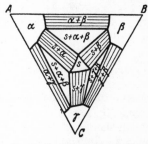

Fɪɢ. 82. Isothermal section in the temperature region of the three binary eutectic crystallizations.

eutectic point *f* (Fig. 76) there appears in the section a two-phase area of solid α and β phases (Fig. 81). Since at this temperature the binary eutectic crystallization of α and β occurs, there is found in this cut a ternary region of α+β+s. The bounding curves of the homogeneous solid solution areas α and β already show a kink, for over one interval these phases stand in equilibrium with each other, and over the remainder of their length coexist with the molten substance. For a temperature underneath the lowest binary point but above the ternary eutectic, the cut shown in Fig. 82 is obtained. On all three sides of the triangle there are binary mixtures of two types of crystals and adjoining them, corresponding three-phase regions. The space of homogeneous melt has been greatly diminished.

At the temperature of the ternary eutectic, the region of the melt has shrunk to a point, and the areas $s+\alpha$, $s+\beta$, and $s+\gamma$, which show primary solidification, to lines. The section is then as depicted in Fig. 75 where z specifies the composition of the eutectic melt. For lower temperatures, as has been explained, the form of the cut is also that given in Fig. 75 except for the disappearance of the melt.

4. Sections Perpendicular to the Plane of Concentration

Of the vertical sections the three indicated in Fig. 83 as Bx, zz', and xy will be studied. As will be seen at once from this figure, the liquidus curve of the section Bx has the form represented in Fig. 84, which shows

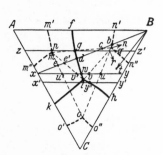

Fig. 83.   Position of the vertical sections xB, zz', and xy.

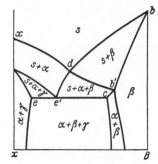

Fig. 84.   Section xB (Fig. 83).

the cusp d corresponding to intersection with the line fl (Fig. 83). From the part dB (Fig. 83) primary β crystallizes out. The vertical section therefore shows, adjacent to the region of the liquid metal, an area of primary crystallization of β. Next to this area there will be, according to the concentration, either the field of homogeneous β solid solution, or that of the binary eutectic crystallization of $\alpha+\beta$. Consequently, the lower boundary of the region of primary crystallization of β is composed of the two curves db' and $b'b$. In the part Bb of Fig. 83 the process of solidification is finished as soon as the primary precipitation of β phase is complete, whereas along db it is continued by the binary eutectic freezing of α and β.

In the case of mechanical mixtures discussed in Chapter II, the path of crystallization could be deduced from the law of conodes because the composition of the substance precipitating out was known, and all conodes extended out from the corners of the concentration triangle. In the present instance the conditions are different. For example, consider the alloy *t* (Fig. 83); it is no longer true that during the precipitation of the β crystals, the composition of the melt is displaced along the projection of the straight line *Bt*. In general, the composition of the melt will deviate to one side or the other of this line (although usually not markedly) as β continues to freeze out, so that for different alloys lying on *Bt* the path of the melt will intersect *hl* at different points. Hence, the line *db'* (Fig. 84) which corresponds to the beginning of the binary eutectic solidification is no longer straight and horizontal but, in general, curved as shown in the figure.

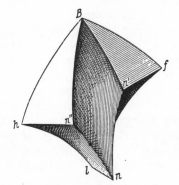

Fig. 78. The state space of primary crystallization (Fig. 76).

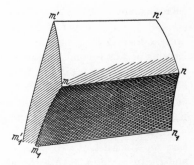

Fig. 79. State space of the mixture of two crystalline types α + β, β + γ, or α + γ (Figs. 75 and 76).

That the area of primary solidification of β actually has the form shown in Fig. 84 follows from an inspection of the space of primary crystallization represented in Fig. 78. The cut being considered passes through the point *B* of this space and also intersects the rib *nn'*, as is evident from Fig. 83. The area so formed has three bounding curves: one against the space of the homogeneous β solid solution (the cut through the surface *n"Bn'n*, Fig. 78), one against the region of binary eutectic solidification of α and β (the intersection of the plane with the surface *nlfn'*), and one against the liquidus surface *lhBf* (which is away from the observer). Whether the curve *b'd* (Fig. 84) descends or ascends in passing from *b'* to *d* depends altogether on the position of the vertical section in relation to the space figure (Fig. 78). If the vertical section is so placed that it intersects *nn'* near *n* and *lf* near *f*, the curve *b'd* will have a position like that shown in Fig. 84. On the other hand, if the section cuts nn' near n' and lf near l, then b' will lie higher than d. The outlines of the area of homogeneous β solid solution are readily deduced from an examination of Fig. 77.

Next consider the line segment bc (Fig. 83) between the intersection of the line Bx with the curve of doubly saturated β solid solution nn' (point b) and its intersection with the boundary rib mn (Fig. 79) located on the surface of the $\alpha + \beta$ region. The alloys along this line must freeze according to the manner of a binary eutectic and finally consist of a mixture of α and β substances. These facts give rise, in Fig. 84, to the area marked $\alpha + \beta$ which adjoins the region of binary eutectic crystallization $\alpha + \beta + s$. The origin of this $\alpha + \beta$ area is made more apparent by examination of the $\alpha + \beta$ space shown in Fig. 79. The plane section Bx cuts successively the curve $n'n$ near n and then the line mn. In this way a piece of the state space $\alpha + \beta$ is cut off in the vicinity of nn_1 and the resulting cross-section appears as in Fig. 84. Between the points c and e (Figs. 83 and 84) the process of solidification terminates in the ternary eutectic point. Left of the point d on the curve fl (Fig. 83), the primary crystallization of α phase first takes place. At the conclusion of this process there next occurs for compositions near d, the binary eutectic freezing of α and β and for alloys near e, a similar precipitation involving α and γ (area $s + \alpha + \gamma$ in Fig. 84). The division between these two types of solidification comes at the point e' on the line ml (Fig. 83). The melt of this particular alloy (e') has already reached the ternary eutectic point upon the completion of the primary solidification of α. From the position of e' on the conode ml, it follows that the alloy at this temperature must consist of two phases having the respective compositions m and l. In conformity with the above facts, Fig. 84 shows the space of primary solidification of α touching the plane of ternary eutectic crystallization at e'.

The field $s + \alpha + \gamma$ must meet the side x at a point, for in the space diagram this space touches the side AC in a straight line. Consequently, at the point x, the eutectic crystallization proceeds at a fixed temperature instead of through a range. The area of primary solidification of α substance differs in form from the β area because the vertical plane encounters the former region along a side instead of in a corner.

Consider next the section zz' (Fig. 83). The curve of primary solidification passes through a minimum value at g (Fig. 85). To the right of g, β precipitates out, and to the left, α. In the portion $z'q$, the process of solidification is completed with the freezing out of the β solid solution. Hence the area of homogeneous β phase adjoins the lower right side of the field of primary crystallization of this substance. Over the interval qr (Fig. 83) a period of binary eutectic crystallization of β and γ follows the primary process. The small region in which this binary solidification occurs is marked $s + \beta + \gamma$ in Fig. 85. Adjoining this region is the area

$r'rqq'$ of the mixture of β and γ solid solutions. The form of this area may be derived from the space diagram shown in Fig. 79 in the same manner as the field $\alpha + \beta$ in Fig. 84 was developed. The horizontal portion of the lower boundary of the region $s + \beta + \gamma$ (Fig. 85) corresponds to the short interval from r to the intersection of zz' with ln (Fig. 83). For the alloy at the point of intersection (not lettered) the primary freezing process for β is followed at once by the ternary eutectic solidification. To the left of this intersection, as far as g, the binary eutectic crystallization of α and β is a feature of solidification. To the left of g, the primary solidification is that of α.

The vertical section cuts the boundary of the region of the mixture of solid solutions α and β at g in Fig. 83. Left of g, the cut remains within the two-phase region, whereas immediately to the right it lies in the field mno of three solid phases. In agreement with this fact, the process of solidification is completed in the interval pg with the binary

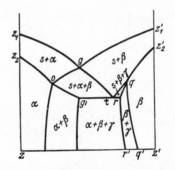

Fig. 85.

Section zz' (Fig. 83).

eutectic crystallization of α and β; hence, the field of the binary mixture of solid α and β is joined directly to the region $s + \alpha + \beta$. On the other hand, as would be anticipated, over gr (Fig. 83) the binary crystallization is followed by the ternary one at the temperature of the line $g'r$. As a consequence of the fact that g stands on the curve fl, the points g and g' have the same composition—that is, the one lies above the other in Fig. 85.

The form of the region of primary crystallization of α and the shape of the field of homogeneous α alloy require no further explanation. The four-cornered shape of the region $s + \alpha + \beta$ in Figs. 84 and 85 originates from the oblique intersection of the vertical plane with the three-cornered tube of binary eutectic crystallization in such a way that besides forming curves of intersection with all three sides of the tube, it also cuts the horizontal plane of ternary eutectic crystallization upon which this tube terminates. The trace of the intersection with this plane provides the fourth boundary, $e'c$, in Fig. 84 and $g't$ in Fig. 85. The fields of $s + \alpha + \gamma$ (Fig. 84) and $s + \beta + \gamma$ (Fig. 85) have simpler forms because the vertical plane cuts the corresponding three-cornered tubes longitudinally. Hence, only two sides of the tube are cut and the traces of these, together with the intersection with the horizontal ternary eutectic plane, provides the three curves forming the boundaries of the fields in question.

There still remains for discussion the field of primary crystallization, $s+\beta$ in Fig. 85. As is evident from the position of zz' (Fig. 83), the vertical plane cuts the space of primary crystallization of β (Fig. 78) in the manner to be described. Upon starting out from the side BC, the vertical plane cuts the surface $nn''Bn'$ (Fig. 78) in the ridge $n''B$ and then encounters the line $n''n$. The trace of $nn''Bn'$ upon the part of the vertical plane included between these two intersections corresponds to the curve z'_2q of Fig. 85. The part of the plane between the intersections with nn'' and ln is represented by rq in Fig. 85. Passing ln, the plane next meets the surface $lfn'n$ (turned away from the observer in Fig. 78) which separates the space of primary crystallization of β from that of

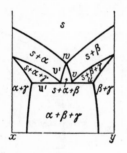

Fig. 86.

Section xy (Fig. 83).

the binary eutectic solidification of α and β, thus generating the curve tg (Fig. 85). The curve gz'_1 is produced by the intersection of the plane with the liquidus surface $hlfB$.

It may be shown that there are cases in which the vertical plane cuts the region of primary crystallization in only two curves.

Let us consider the section xy (Fig. 86). To the right of the point w where this section cuts the curve fl, the primary crystallization of β occurs and to the left, that of α. Correspondingly, the liquidus line in Fig. 86 has two parts which meet at w. No field of homogeneous solid solution appears in this section since the vertical plane does not cross any such space. All compositions between v and the right side of the diagram undergo the binary eutectic solidification of β and γ together as soon as the primary precipitation of β material has been completed. The alloys to the right of u become completely solidified during the binary eutectic process whereas those lying to the left as far as u' experience the ternary eutectic crystallization. In the interval uv, the binary eutectic crystallization of β and γ is followed by the ternary eutectic process. Over the interval vv' the ternary process is preceded by the precipitation of α and β simultaneously, whereas between v' and u' it comes at the completion of the binary eutectic crystallization of the α and γ substances. The left side of Fig. 86 is very similar to the right and needs no explanation.

The region of primary crystallization has a simpler form here than in Fig. 85 because the plane has no contact with the fields of homogeneous solid solution, and therefore no curves of the type of qz'_2 appear. A still simpler case occurs if the section does not pass through the region of binary eutectic crystallization of α and β, as in the sections $x'y'$, parallel to the side AB but passes between C and the point l (Fig. 83). In this section only the eutectic solidification of β and γ follows the primary crystallization of β. At the point, y'', where the vertical plane cuts the curve hl, the binary crystallization begins directly from the melt. The points v and w (Fig. 86) have thus moved to coincidence. In the middle portion of the section $x'y'$, the primary crystallization of γ occurs; hence, the liquidus line consists of three portions.

In the cases under discussion, the sections have been derived primarily from consideration of the space diagram. It is also possible to proceed, as mentioned in Chapter II, by following the changes in the concentration of the various phases during freezing and drawing conclusions therefrom concerning the manner of crystallization. For example, it would be agreed from a consideration of the cut xy that during the precipitation of β the melt becomes continually poorer in this phase, and for any initial composition on the interval yv is displaced toward AC until the curve hl is encountered. From here on, both β and γ are precipitated in a binary eutectic crystallization in which the compositions of the melt and of the β and γ crystals move respectively along the lines hl, $n''n$, and $o''o$ from right to left. Because of the precipitation of the β and γ solid solutions, the melt is gradually consumed. If the alloy lies between y and u, solidification will be completed before the melt becomes saturated in the α constituent—that is, during the binary eutectic crystallization. If the mean composition of the alloy is between u and v, the melt will attain the composition l and solidification will be finished by the ternary eutectic crystallization. It is instructive and is recommended to the reader to analyze other parts of this section as well as other sections of this diagram in a similar manner. By what method one arrives at the construction of the diagram is immaterial. In order to avoid errors, it is recommended to check frequently one method by the other.

Chapter VII

Systems with Solubility Gaps in the Liquid State

A. Liquid State

It has hitherto been assumed that metals in the liquid state are soluble in each other in all proportions. However, in many important metal systems the constituents are soluble in each other in the liquid state to only a limited degree. Examples are the lead-containing copper alloys and the systems lead-zinc, lead-aluminum, and so on.

Before taking up the question of solubility gaps in the liquid state, the relations in one-component and binary systems should be reviewed.

Although a continuous transition from the anisotropic crystalline phase to the liquid or vapor form cannot be assumed, such a change does proceed between the fluid and gaseous states. It is well known that by

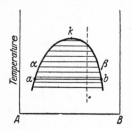

Fig. 87.

Gap in miscibility in the liquid state in a binary system.

the application of a sufficiently high pressure, the transformation from the liquid to the vapor state as the temperature rises may be caused to take place in a continuous manner. For one-component systems there is a definite temperature and pressure at which the vapor and liquid phases become identical. At this point, the temperature is called the "critical temperature" and the pressure, the "critical pressure."

In many two-component systems there exists two liquids which possess only a limited degree of solubility in each other. For a rising temperature the gap in miscibility in such a system generally becomes narrower and vanishes altogether at a temperature called the "critical temperature" of the system. At this temperature the two liquids which previously existed separately merge into a single, homogeneous phase. Such a system is illustrated in Fig. 87 where k is the critical point. Below the temperature of k, the two components A and B are only partially miscible in the fluid state; hence, two liquids coexist—α, rich in A, and β, rich in B; akb is the region of immiscibility. The two curves, ak and bk, meet at k to form a continuous curve and as a consequence, the compositions of both phases change very rapidly in the vicinity of this point. Above k no gap in miscibility exists. Fig. 87 represents the situation for one definite pressure below the vapor pressure; similar curves in different positions exist for other pressures. At low pressures the components may pass into the vapor phase before the liquids become miscible.

The point k lies at a critical temperature and critical composition. If a melt of some different composition is cooled until the temperature reaches a point on the boundary curve akb, a second phase will be precipitated. This new phase will have the composition corresponding to the opposite end of the conode which passes through the first point. If the melt has the composition k, the liquid simply divides into two portions as soon as the temperature drops to the critical value. The reverse process takes place on heating.

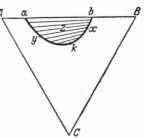

Fig. 88.

    Isothermal section through a region of immiscibility in the liquid state in a ternary system.

The phases represented by the points a and b at the ends of the horizontal line ab (Fig. 87) are in equilibrium with each other and lie at the same temperature. These horizontal lines are called "conodes" for they are of the same type as those described in Chapter I.

The manner in which the concentrations of the two mutually saturated phases change with temperature is very complex. Cases exist in which the critical point lies at a low temperature, and a separation of the homogeneous liquid into two immiscible ones occurs as the temperature rises. This last case will not be discussed further. Instead, it will be supposed that the immiscibility appears as the temperature is lowered and that the gap becomes wider if the temperature drops farther.

The consideration of ternary systems may now be taken up. Assume that at some temperature one of the binary systems—e.g., AB—has a miscibility gap, ab, in the liquid state (Fig. 88) but that the other two have complete miscibility in the liquid condition.

The miscibility gap must be closed inside the ternary system. To

each point on the curve ak—for example, the point y—there corresponds
a point x on bk which gives the composition of the second liquid phase
which is in equilibrium with the first. Hence, xy is a conode. The entire
solubility gap may be considered to have conodes passing across it. Upon
approaching the point where the gap in solubility is closed, the conodes
become continually shorter and finally shrink to zero length. At this
point the two coexisting liquids have identical compositions and merge
into a single phase. The point k at which the two phases merge is
called the "critical point" for this case.

The position and size of the gap, akb, is displaced with temperature.
For each temperature at which the break in solubility exists, there will
be a "partial" critical point, k. If the assemblage of such section diagrams
is developed into a space diagram the result will be as shown in Fig. 89.

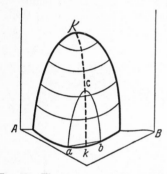

Fig. 89. The state space of a mixture
of two liquids in a ternary system.
The critical point lies in the binary
system AB.

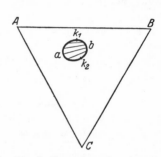

Fig. 90. Isothermal section through a
region of immiscibility in the liquid
state with the critical point inside
of the ternary system.

The combination of akb curves gives a kind of vault or partial dome which
diminishes in size toward the top—if, as assumed here, the gap in solubility narrows with rising temperature. If the gap always becomes
narrower as it leaves the side AB to extend into the interior of the ternary
system, the dome will lean against the side AB of the prism of state.
That is, the dome is cut off by the prism side before its zenith has been
reached.

If a line kK is drawn through the continuum of critical points which
exist on the isothermal sections at successively higher temperatures, it
must end in the critical point K, which lies in the binary system (equivalent to k in Fig. 87). This point K will accordingly be the highest point
of the curve kK, which is called the "critical curve."

Let us consider a point, z, inside the region of limited miscibility
(Fig. 88). The conode which connects the two liquid phases into which
an alloy of composition z breaks up, must pass through z regardless of

the temperature being considered. However, the succession of conodes which pass through z as the temperature rises will not, in general, lie in a vertical plane, for the surface generated, if the series of conodes is considered as a single conode which ascends as the temperature rises, is a screw surface which rotates about a vertical axis Z through z. The degree by which this screw surface deviates from a plane is usually small.

We shall next consider a consequence of the form of the conode surface described in the previous paragraph. Assume that the region of immiscible liquids (Fig. 89) is cut by a vertical plane so placed that the zenith, c, of the curve of intersection lies on the critical curve kK. The curve of intersection acb will then appear similar to a hyperbola. The fact to be observed is that two points on acb which lie at the same temperature will not be the ends of conodes.

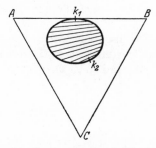

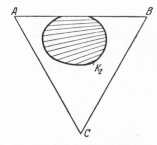

Fig. 91. Section like that in Fig. 90 at a lower temperature. The gap of immiscibility touches the binary system AB.

Fig. 92. Section similar to Fig. 91 at a still lower temperature.

The break in solubility need not necessarily lie so that for all temperatures it extends out from a binary system and is closed off inside the ternary system. It may originate within the ternary system. Consider such a case beginning at a temperature above the dome of the region of immiscibility. When the temperature has dropped a little below the top of the immiscibility space, an isothermal section appears as shown in Fig. 90. The section ak_1bk_2 of the dome lies entirely within the triangle and has two critical points, k_1 and k_2, at which the two phases in equilibrium with each other become identical. As the temperature is lowered further, the region of immiscibility widens and touches one side of the triangle—for example, AB (Fig. 91). It is easy to see that the point of tangency of the boundary of the gap against the side of the prism of state must be a partial critical point if a contradiction is to be avoided. For still lower temperatures, the form of section shown in Fig. 92 is obtained. This diagram does not differ in any essential way from the one exhibited in Fig. 88.

As shown in the preceding paragraphs the zenith of the dome-like space of immiscibility lies within the interior of the prism of state. The critical curve passes through this point and runs down both sides. Below, the space of immiscibility, if not closed off by an inverted dome, will be bounded by the region of solidification.

It is obvious that the form of the region of two immiscible liquids is very simple so long as only the space in which the alloy is liquid is considered.

B. Mechanical Mixture without the Formation of Solid Solution and with a Gap in Solubility in the Liquid State which does not Intersect any Eutectic Curve

1. Process of Crystallization. State Spaces

We next take up the consideration of crystallization of alloys in regions of immiscibility in the fluid state. By way of introduction, the behavior in binary diagrams will be studied first. The discussion will be limited to the simplest case, which is the mechanical mixture without the formation of solid solutions and without compounds. In Fig. 93 there is shown

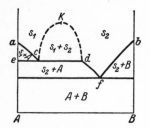

Fig. 93.

Solidification diagram of a binary system with a gap of solubility in the liquid state.

such a binary system with a gap in solubility in the fluid alloys. The process of solidification takes place in the following manner: From the molten alloys with compositions in the interval ac, constituent A crystallizes out in the normal way. When the melt has reached the composition of the point c, a second liquid phase, d, is also precipitated. For constant pressure, the system is now invariant, since it consists of three phases —namely, two melts and the solid constituent, A. There occurs therefore at constant temperature the reaction: $c \rightarrow A + d$ until all the melt c is consumed. After the completion of this reaction, the composition of the melt moves along the curve df while component A is precipitated in the normal manner. If the composition of the alloy lies between c and d, the process of freezing differs from that just described only in that it begins with the invariant reaction. If the composition is to the right of d, the gap in solubility is without influence on the process of solidification.

An essential fact in the above example is that during solidification there comes into existence a new kind of invariant equilibrium characterized by the presence of two liquid phases. The presence of the three phases demands that the line cd be isothermal.

Consideration of the ternary system will now be taken up and the assumption made that the region of immiscibility in the liquid state has the form illustrated in Figs. 88 and 89, in which the gap in solubility becomes narrower as the distance from the side increases. It will further be assumed that the eutectic curves gl, hl, and kl lie outside the region of immiscibility (Fig. 94). Hence, as the temperature drops, the region

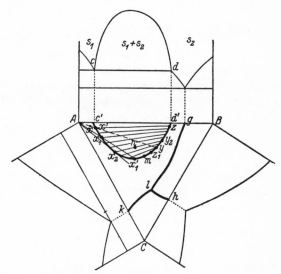

Fig. 94. Triangle of concentrations of a mechanical mixture having in the liquid state a solubility gap which does not cut a eutectic curve.

of immiscibility must somewhere encounter the surface of the beginning of crystallization of A. To make the case more definite, suppose that the curve marking the intersection of this immiscibility dome with the surface of the crystallization of A is $c'md'$ (Fig. 94). This curve has a different significance from akb in Fig. 88, for the latter simply represents an isothermal section through the region of immiscibility, whereas $c'md'$ is the trace of the immiscibility dome on the liquidus surface of A. Whether $c'md'$ has all its points at constant temperature is one of the items to be investigated.

Let us consider the process of freezing of melt x, which is so placed that the line Ax, when extended, strikes the previously mentioned curve $c'md'$.

The solidification will begin in the normal manner, as described in Chapter II, by the crystallization of A out of the melt. As a consequence, the composition of the melt moves along the projection of the line Ax until it intersects the curve $c'md'$ in the point x'. At this stage, a second liquid phase appears. As an experiment, its composition will first be supposed to lie on the extension of the line Ax at the point y. The relationship between x' and its decomposition products will then be: $x' \rightarrow A + y$.

This reaction must obviously proceed in an invariant manner for geometric reasons. During a reaction proceeding in either direction, the composition of the phase x' must not change in such a way as to depart from the line Ay, nor may the phase y leave it. The fact may also be seen from the viewpoint of phase theory. On the line Ay, the ratio of the amount of B to the amount of C is constant (see Chapter I, Section 2). Because of the requirement that all three phases must lie on a straight line, one composition variable is lost. The system has only two independent constituents because only the amount of A, and the amount of either B or C can be changed independently on account of the fixed ratio between B and C.

The above analysis reveals that an unnecessary restriction has been made, since in a three-component system at constant pressure, four phases may coexist in an invariant equilibrium, and the pronouncement of the phase rule is important exactly because it specifies that the theoretically possible degree of complexity must actually be realized.

This limitation can be removed immediately by dropping the assumption that the second liquid phase lies on the extension of the line Ax'. Let us assume that the composition lies at some other point—for example, at z. In this way a three-phase triangle $Ax'z$ is obtained which has similarities to the triangle of the binary eutectic solidification described in Chapter II. Actually, the behavior is quite similar throughout, except that in Chapter II only one phase, the melt, had variable composition whereas in the present case there are two liquid phases, x' and z, of which the composition can vary.

When the second liquid phase begins to form from the mixture of A and x', the composition of the latter must be displaced along the boundary curve toward m, for this curve specifies the compositions of the phases contributing to the three-phase equilibrium. The concentration point, x, must be in the interior of the three-phase triangle. The temperature must fall, since there is still one degree of freedom, in exactly the same way as it does for binary eutectic solidification. This fact implies that along the curve $c'x'm$ the temperature must decrease in the direction from c' toward m. Also, the composition of the point z must change with diminishing temperature and must, in fact, move along the boundary curve $d'zm$ in the direction from d' toward m.

It is clear that the points x' and z on the bounding curve must be at the same temperature, since the corresponding phases are in equilibrium with each other; hence, the line $x'z$ is a conode. As the three-phase reaction proceeds, corresponding to each temperature there will be a pair of points on the curves $c'x'm$ and $d'zm$, and these points will constitute the end points of conodes. Several such conodes are indicated schematically in Fig. 94. From the above discussion, it follows at once that the surface $c'md'$ really constitutes a part of the liquidus surface of component A. It is generated by the gliding of an isothermal line down the branches $c'm$ and $d'm$ of the curve $c'md'$.

In binary systems, a reaction between two melts and one solid form is designated as "monotectic." In ternary systems, as will be seen later, there may be similar reactions and in addition those in which two solid phases participate (such reactions are invariant). A reaction of the type described above will be called a "monotectic three-phase reaction."

In what manner will the monotectic three-phase reaction in the above case be completed? The answer depends upon the mutual positions of the points x', y, and z and the displacements of x' and z. If the displacement is such that the composition of the second melt reaches the second intersection of the line Ax with the boundary curve (y, in the present case), the alloy, x, will then consist only of the solid form, A, and the liquid phase, y, while the first liquid phase will have been used up. The system no longer possesses three phases but has returned to a two-phase equilibrium between A and y. The further solidification of A will proceed therefore in the normal manner by the movement of the composition of the melt along the extension of the line Axy as A is precipitated. This process will continue until the melt encounters the line gl and the binary eutectic crystallization of A and B begins. There is no need for giving further details since the process of solidification is exactly like that described in Chapter II.

Next, suppose that the composition of the alloy is such that its representative point lies on the line Ax_1. During the monotectic ternary reaction the melt lying on the x branch of the boundary moves around to the point x'_1 lying on the extension Ax'_1 of Ax_1, while the melt on the z branch still lies on the d' side of m, with the result that the latter is consumed first. Then, as further solidification takes place, the composition of the remaining melt will move along the extension of the line Ax'_1 in the direction toward line gl. Obviously there must be an intermediate composition such that neither melt is consumed first, but the two liquids merge. This point of mergence, m, must have the significance of a critical point, since the two phases of limited solubility become identical. It is clear that this condition can be fulfilled only for alloys whose compositions lie on the line Am, m being the critical point. In this case, the monotectic ternary reaction does not end by the disappearance of one of the liquid phases but by the mergence of both. Further solidification takes place through the precipitation of A in the usual manner.

Is is also clear that m lies at the temperature minimum of the curve $c'md'$. If some other point, y, were the minimum, then for a point such as z_1, lying between y and m, it would be impossible to find a corresponding point at the same temperature on the portion $c'm$ which would represent a melt in equilibrium with the first one. A point in equilibrium with z_1 could be found only in the interval yd'. This result is a contradiction of the original assumption, since the critical point was defined as being between the two liquid phases of limited mutual solubility.

From the above analysis an idea has been gained of the boundary curve, $c'md'$, of the intersection of the region of immiscibility and the liquidus surface on which A is precipitated. This curve sinks away from c' and d' toward the inner part of the triangle, and its point of lowest

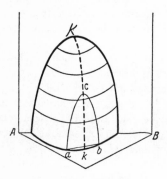

FIG. 89.

The state space of a mixture of two liquids in a ternary system. The critical point lies in the binary system AB.

temperature coincides with the critical point m. This point m also lies on the critical curve kK (Fig. 89), situated on the surface of the dome of the region of immiscibility.

If the concentration of an alloy is such that it lies within the region of limited solubility, its behavior on cooling will differ from the cases just discussed only by having the monotectic three-phase reaction begin as soon as the temperature has fallen to the point where solidification sets in. No other process occurs since the alloy already consists of two liquid phases. For example, suppose the alloy n (Fig. 94) before the beginning of the precipitation of crystals of A consists of the melts x_2 and y_2 in amounts determined by the law of levers. During solidification the three-phase triangle Ax_2y_2 is displaced by having the side x_2y_2 in Fig. 94 back downward away from the point of alloy composition. The process of monotectic three-phase reaction in this case differs in no way from that described previously for the alloy x. The solidification of all alloys whose compositions lie outside the line Ax_2, which is the tangent to the curve $c'md'$ passing through A, is not influenced by the existence of the solubility gap in the liquid state, since this gap does not lie on their paths of solidification.

It is now possible to depict the form of the state space which arises through the solidification process. The region of liquid immiscibility, which has a form similar to that shown in Fig. 89, rests upon the liquidus surface of the component A and its line of intersection with this surface is the curve $c'md'$ (Fig. 94). This surface is generated, as has been mentioned, through the movement of the line $c'd'$ along the curves $c'm$ and $d'm$. At m the moving line reaches the boundary curve of this surface —that is, it becomes tangent to the curve $c'md'$.

Above the surface $c'md'$, the alloys consist of two liquid phases, s_1 and s_2. According to the general rule (see supplement to Chapter II) this space must adjoin either a one-phase or a three-phase space. In the present instance, the space below must be a three-phase one, since the precipitation of the component A begins as soon as the state point of the alloy reaches the surface $c'md'$. The monotectic reaction between the two melts, s_1 and s_2, and the solid material A must correspond to a state space of which the form can be pictured most easily by following the motion of the three-phase triangle $Ax'z$ (Fig. 94). As has been noted in other systems, the phase triangle degenerates to a straight line on the side of the prism of state ($c'd'$ on side AB). The corner x of this triangle advances from the side into the interior of the triangular prism and traces a skew curve $c'm$ (actually a kind of rib) upon the surface of the space of monotectic equilibrium. It is characteristic of spaces in which there exist partially miscible phases with critical points that two sides of the three-phase triangle, as Az and Ax', approach each other and coincide at a point, as m. The boundaries of the three-phase space may be described in the following manner. The upper boundary is the surface $c'md'$, which is generated by the movement of the conode line. Upon one side the space rests against the binary system AB. The boundary surface, which is the most interesting, is the one generated by the displacement of an isothermal straight line, one end of which lies on the point A and hence can move only in the vertical direction, and the other, starting at the point c', follows along the boundary curve through x' and m around to d'.

Since the points c' and d' lie at the same temperature, the phase space $s_1 + s_2 + A$ touches the side AB only at the one isothermal line, and hence is completely closed thereby. It has the form of an assay crucible lying on its side. The end at A is drawn out in the vertical direction and the sides are formed by the curved surface generated by the horizontal line passing through A. Where the crucible touches the side AB its surface exhibits a horizontal (isothermal) crease. The open end of the crucible is outlined by the boundary curve $c'md'$.

This crucible-shaped form produces in the state space of the primary crystallization of A, a region which prevents the (theoretically impossible) direct contact of the space of two liquid phases, $s_1 + s_2$, with the space of primary crystallization of A by the insertion of a three-phase region, $s_1 + s_2 + A$, between these two two-phase regions. Also, for alloys in the partial region $Ac'x_2$ it separates the two regions of primary crystallization of A from each other. This space is thus surrounded on all sides except over the surface $c'md'$ by the space of primary solidification of A, and for this reason does not stand out in the ordinary perspective picture.

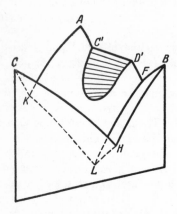

Fig. 95.

Space diagram corresponding to Fig. 94.

Fig. 95 shows a view of the combined spaces of monotectic reaction and primary solidification of A. The three-phase region extends out from $c'md'$.

The remaining state spaces of this system correspond to those of the mechanical mixture (Chapter II).

2. Isothermal Sections

We shall now attempt, through consideration first of isothermal and then of vertical sections, to develop a completely understandable picture of the process of solidification. In Fig. 96 is shown an isothermal section at a temperature below the beginning of the precipitation of A, but above the initiation of the monotectic three-phase reaction. (The assumption has been made that the two liquid phases already exist.) This section consists of the small region of primary solidification of A and the melt which in the area $s_1 + s_2$ consists of two liquids of limited solubility.

Fig. 97 represents conditions during the period when the monotectic three-phase reaction is in process. The region Axz is the section of the three-phase space made by the plane under consideration. It will be noted that this area has already moved away from the side AB. In the region $Ad'z$ the primary solidification process has been resumed after completion of the monotectic reaction. It is evident that the three-phase region $s_1 + s_2 + A$ is not directly in contact with the homogeneous melt but is separated from it by the two-phase space s_1+s_2. The downward-moving isothermal plane encounters this region before intersecting the three-phase space, s_1+s_2+A.

The suggestion of two different liquid phases, s_1 and s_2, in the phase field of the homogeneous liquid in Figs. 96 and 97 can have a meaning

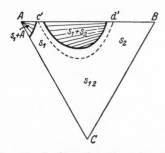

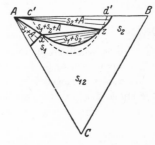

FIG. 96. Isothermal section after the beginning of solidification of A.

FIG. 97. Isothermal section after the formation of a three-phase field involving two melts.

only in a restricted sense. The two liquids merge into each other and actually constitute the homogeneous region s. Such a dual designation is an outgrowth of the concept of a critical point. In recognition of this peculiarity, the melt in its vicinity is marked with a double index (s_{12}). Below the three-phase region, the process of solidification is no longer affected by the gap in solubility.

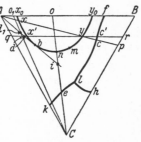

FIG. 98.

Position of the vertical sections Ap, qr, Co, and Co_1.

In Figs. 96 and 97 the crystallization of the other two components is not considered since no new features would be introduced by considering them.

3. Vertical Sections

The four vertical sections designated as Ap, qr, Co, and Co_1 in Fig. 98, may be selected for discussion. In the interval Ax of the cut Ap (Fig. 99) the primary solidification of A occurs first. The interval xy corresponds to the region of the two liquid phases. Along yc, the precipitation of A from a single liquid phase is resumed. The primary solidification of A in all alloys in the interval Ax is followed, beginning at the temperature of the point x, by the monotectic reaction between this component and the two liquid phases s_1 and s_2. Hence, the region $s_1 + A$ is separated from the three-phase space $s_1 + s_2 + A$ below it by the isothermal straight line $a'x$. A straight isothermal line also bounds the bottom of the latter region, which is the field of the monotectic reaction. The end of this reaction is reached, for all alloys having compositions to the left of y, when the phase x has been consumed and the molten substance is composed of y alone. The form of this three-phase area might also have been deduced from the knowledge that the boundary surface in the space diagram was generated by the motion of an isothermal line of which one end passed through A. As the temperature drops further,

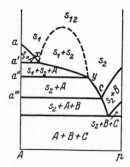

Fig. 99. Section Ap (Fig. 98).

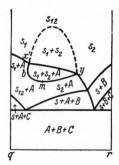

Fig. 100. Section qr (Fig. 98).

the region of primary solidification of A is again encountered. From this point on, the freezing process goes on as described in Chapter II, and no further description is required.

Next consider the cut qr (Fig. 100). In the interval from q to d, the latter being the point of intersection of the plane with the tangent Ab to the region of two liquid phases, the path of the melt is not affected by the presence of the gap in miscibility. The region of immiscibility can affect only those compositions lying between d and y, and in this interval a three-phase area with two liquid melts is encountered during the freezing process. The upper boundary of this area is the line of intersection of the vertical plane with the surface generated by the motion of a conode over the curve produced by the meeting of the immiscibility dome and the liquidus surface. The point x' is at a higher temperature than y since it lies on a higher conode. However, the difference in temperature between these points is less than that between x and y (Fig. 99). The lower boundary of this region can be imagined most simply by consider-

ing that it is produced by the intersection of the plane qr with the path
of the isothermal line which passes through A and the points of the curve
$x'bmy$.

Over the interval dx' the three-phase region will be reached, as the
alloy cools out of the space of the primary crystallization of A, whenever
the conode arrow passing through A meets the boundary curve at some
point in the portion $x'b$. Since the point b is at a lower temperature than
x', the boundary curve has the form bx' shown in Fig. 100. The alloys of
the part $x'y$ encounter the three-phase region upon cooling below the
space of two liquids. They leave this region as soon as one of the liquid
phases is exhausted. In the interval $x'm$ the first liquid phase to be
consumed will be s_2 whereas in the part my it will be s_1, m being the critical point (Fig. 100). The curve bmy corresponds to these changes.
The point m, since it is the critical point, must lie at the lowest tempera-

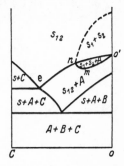

Fig. 101.

Section Co (Fig. 98).

ture. For this reason, the lower boundary curve of the monotectic field
must drop away from y to lower temperatures if the cut is so taken that
m lies between b and y. No discontinuity occurs at the point b (Fig.
100), since $x'bmy$ (Fig. 98) is a continuous curve.

Let us next consider the cut Co (Fig. 98). In the partial region Ce, the
component C crystallizes out first (Fig. 101). Along en, A is the first solid
component to appear. In neither interval does the gap of insolubility have
any influence. Over no, the cooling alloys pass through the region of
limited miscibility corresponding to two liquid layers, and as soon as they
leave it, experience the monotectic reaction which occurs in the space $s_1 +
s_2 + A$. The upper boundary of the area of this reaction (no', Fig. 101) is
produced by the intersection of the vertical plane with the surface $c'md'$
(Fig. 94). As already described in connection with the cut qr, the alloy
will pass downward through the lower boundary of this area when one of
the two liquid layers is consumed and the composition of the other has
reached the second intersection of the conode through A (and, naturally,
through the representative point of the alloy) with the boundary curve

$c'md'$. It is further obvious that the temperature of the points in the lower boundary of this region decreases as the composition changes from o to the alloy whose conode passes through m and thereafter increases. Again, the point m corresponds to the lowest temperature of the curve nmo' (Fig. 101). Further solidification follows in the customary manner for mechanical mixtures and does not require description.

If the section is taken so that it meets the curve x_0bmy_0 (Fig. 98) to the left of b, the only difference from Fig. 101 is that the region s_1+s_2+A, beginning at point n, experiences a bulge on the left side similar to that shown in Fig. 100. A more exact determination of the form of the section will be left to the reader.

On the section Co_1, which does not meet the region of the immiscible liquids, precipitation of either A or C begins in the normal manner over the entire length (Fig. 102). The alloys in the interval d_1o_1 move tem-

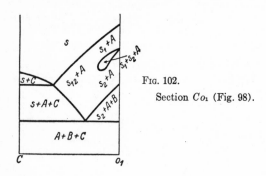

Fig. 102.

Section Co_1 (Fig. 98).

porarily into the region s_1+s_2+A as solidification proceeds. The boundary curve of the three-phase area is simply the cross-section made by the vertical plane passing through the crucible-shaped region described above. The discontinuity on this boundary which was shown at n in Fig. 101 has disappeared, since the three-phase field is entirely surrounded by the one state space, $s+A$.

C.   Gap in Solubility in the
Liquid State Interrupts a Eutectic Curve

1.   Process of Crystallization.   State Spaces

It is well known that in a binary system of the mechanical mixture type which exhibits a gap in solubility in the liquid state, the eutectic cannot occur in the gap. If the eutectic did occur within the field of two incompletely miscible liquids, four phases—two solid and two liquid— would exist simultaneously, a condition which would be in violation of the phase rule, which specifies that only three phases can exist in equilibrium in a binary system. Since in a ternary system there is one more degree of freedom, this difficulty disappears and the possibility of a binary eutectic solidification occurring in the presence of two liquid layers actually exists. This case will now be examined.

Let it be assumed that the position of the gap in solubility is such that the curve of the melt saturated in both A and C—line ki in Fig. 103—runs into it. The question may now be put concerning the manner in which solidification occurs under such circumstances. The alloys with compositions in the field Aik will first be considered. After the primary crystallization of A is completed, these alloys undergo a binary solidification of A and C together, during which the composition of the melt moves along ki. Upon reaching i, the curve encounters a region where greater complication exists. The melt i finds itself in equilibrium with another melt, j, which lies on the opposite side of the gap and at the same temperature, ij

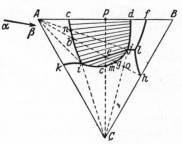

Fig. 103.

Triangle of concentrations of a mechanical mixture having in the liquid state a gap in solubility which intersects a eutectic curve.

being the conode which connects the two melts. The system of four phases —two solid, A and C, and two liquid, i and j—must be invariant. Hence, it can exist at only the one temperature, and furthermore the reaction which occurs can change only the amount of the phases but not their composition. It is at once evident that the arrangement of the individual state points in Fig. 103 corresponds to the invariant eutectic case (compare Chapter I) and that the reaction which occurs must result in the formation or decomposition of the melt i: $i \rightleftarrows A + C + j$. Such a reaction is designated as a monotectic four-phase reaction. For an extraction of heat, the crystallization of A and C occurs, or the reaction runs from left to right. As soon as the melt i is exhausted, the system consists of only the three phases A, C, and j. The binary eutectic crystallization can now resume its progress. The melt moves along jl to the ternary eutectic point l at which all three of the components are precipitated simultaneously.

The solidification of the alloys of the field Cik is accomplished in the same manner, except that there is a primary crystallization of C, not of A. The two regions of binary eutectic crystallization of A and C are separated by a plane of invariant equilibrium resulting from the presence of the two liquid layers.

Freezing of the alloys in the triangle Ain takes place in the following manner: Some time after the melt has begun to precipitate component A, its composition reaches a point on the interval ni. There then begins in the same way as described in the previous section, the formation of a second liquid phase having a composition represented by a point or the line dj. More exactly, the composition of this new phase is at the opposite end of the conode which passes through the composition of the first phase. During the monotectic reaction which occurs, the amount of the melt lying on ni decreases while the quantity of the liquid phase on the interval dj becomes greater and, simultaneously, the crystallization of A proceeds. The temperature drops during this period and continues to do so as the reaction continues, and the two melts move along the two boundary curves until they reach the points i and j, respectively. Both are then saturated in both A and C, and from this point on solidification progresses as it did for the alloys of the region AiC—that is, the invariant reaction between the four phases A, C, i, and j takes place. After the conclusion of this reaction, the binary solidification of A and C is continued with lowering temperature as the melt moves along the curve jl.

In the partial region Anc, the first melt is consumed before the point i is reached and also before the second melt reaches j in passing down the curve dj during the monotectic ternary reaction. After the melt of interval cn is exhausted, the primary crystallization of A is resumed, and upon its completion there occurs the binary eutectic solidification of either A and C or of A and B together, depending upon the composition of the alloy. The solidification of the alloys in this area takes place in exactly the same manner as in the case described in section B.

The freezing of the alloys lying in the field $ciejd$ differs from the process just described only because the separation into two liquid layers occurs before solidification begins, and consequently the monotectic three-phase reaction starts simultaneously with the crystallizing process. The three-phase reaction is followed either by the primary solidification of A or by the monotectic four-phase reaction.

It has been assumed that the region of two liquids extends beyond the eutectic curve ki and has some such boundary as the curve imj. The two points i and j lie at the same temperature since they are the end points of a conode. Since the liquidus surface on which C begins to be precipitated slopes downward toward ki and jl, the curve imj, which is the line of intersection of this surface with the dome-like region of two immiscible liquids, must rise to higher temperatures as it leaves i and j. Exactly the same considerations which in the previous section demonstrated that the critical point, m, lay at the minimum temperature, show that in the present instance it corresponds to the highest temperature on the curve.

As the solidification of the alloys in the region $Cimj$ proceeds with the crystallizing out of C, the composition of the melt eventually reaches a point on the curve imj. If the composition of the melt reaches a point to the left of m, there is formed a new liquid phase of which the representative point lies on the interval mj. On the other hand, if it reaches a point to the right of m, the new liquid phase has a composition represented by a point on im. If the composition of the alloy is on the line joining m and C, the path of the melt will reach the point m and the hitherto homogeneous melt will separate into two liquid phases. This change occurs in the usual manner experienced by a cooling melt when it strikes a critical point on the surface of a space within which two liquid phases exist. During the monotectic reaction which now sets in, the crystallization of C takes place, accompanied by a drop in temperature, while the two liquids move along the boundary curve toward i and j, respectively. When they reach these points, the precipitation of A begins. The system thus enters the stage of the previously described monotectic four-phase equilibrium in which the reaction proceeds, as stated before, until the melt i is ex-

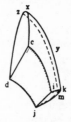

Fig. 104.

State space of the region of immiscibility (Fig. 103).

hausted, whereupon the simple binary eutectic crystallization of A and C begins. For the alloys having compositions in the part $imje$ of the region of immiscibility, the three-phase reaction starts simultaneously with the beginning of solidification.

It is now possible to take up the form of the state spaces which develop during the freezing process. The lower boundary, $cimjd$, of the space of two liquid phases consists of two parts. In part $icdj$, the temperature decreases in going from c toward i and from d toward j. In part imj, the temperature rises in going from i and j toward m; ij is an isothermal rib on the lower surface of the two-liquid state space. This state space has the form shown in Fig. 104 when viewed from below in the direction of the arrow $\alpha\beta$. The face, dxc, lies in the binary system AB; $xynjd$ is the hidden portion of the upper and side boundary surface of the space, and $dcimj$ is the previously mentioned two-part under surface; mz is the critical curve which lies on the part hidden from the observer. This curve intersects the curve cxd at the point of maximum temperature, z.

Adjoining the underside of the space just described are two monotectic three-phase spaces, one having two liquids and the solid A, and the other with two liquids and the crystalline C. The outlines of the first are obtained in a manner similar to that used to deduce the form of the crucible-shaped space described in the previous section, but with the additional consideration that in this instance the lower boundary is an isothermal plane. The situation may be described by saying that the monotectic

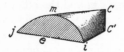

Fig. 105.

State space of $s_1 + s_2 + C$.

three-phase reaction is prematurely stopped by the occurrence of the invariant four-phase reaction. It will be seen further on how this condition affects the diagrams obtained by taking vertical sections .

The three-phase space, in which the crystalline C is in equilibrium with two liquid phases, has the form illustrated in Fig. 105 when viewed in the direction of the arrow (Fig. 103). Its upper boundary is generated by the movement of an isothermal line passing through C and moving along the boundary line imj; below, it is limited by the partial plane jCi (Fig. 103) of the monotectic invariant equilibrium.

Of the remaining state spaces, none have properties which have not already been covered in Chapter II.

2. Isothermal Sections

Let us assume that the component A has the highest melting point. So long as the region of primary crystallization of this component does not

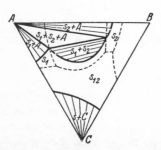

Fig. 106. Isothermal section after the beginning of solidification of A and C (Fig. 103).

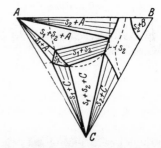

Fig. 107. Isothermal section after separation of the fields of concentration of the two melts.

encounter the space of two liquids, no complication arises; hence there is no need to consider an isothermal section at these temperatures.

In Fig. 106 is shown an isothermal section which cuts the three-phase space of the two liquids s_1 and s_2 and the solid A, but does not involve C

in the three-phase reaction. The outlines of the areas of crystallization
of A correspond very closely to those shown in Fig. 97. At this temperature the crystallization of C proceeds from one liquid in the normal manner. The section shown in Fig. 107 corresponds to a lower temperature
at which there is a three-phase equilibrium of C with two liquids. The
triangle $s_1 + s_2 + C$ corresponds to a horizontal section through the state
space shown in Fig. 105. Between the two monotectic three-phase regions
lies the area of two liquids. The binary eutectic crystallization of A and C
has already begun. Fig. 108 corresponds to the temperature of the conode
ij (Fig. 103). The two three-phase regions having two liquids and also

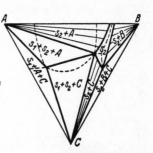

Fig. 108.

   Isothermal section shortly before
the completion of solidification.

the region of binary eutectic crystallization of A and C along the left have
all met together. They reveal the form of the four-phase quadrilateral.
After melt s_1 has been consumed, the three triangles $s_1 + s_2 + A$, $s_1 + s_2 + C$,
and $s_1 + A + C$ are replaced by the one triangle $s_2 + A + C$ and the binary
eutectic crystallization proceeds in the normal manner.

3. Vertical Sections

The sections passing through A but missing the conode ij present no
situations different from those discussed in section B. In Fig. 109 is
shown the cut Ah (Fig. 103) which follows the line passing through
component A and the eutectic in the binary system BC. In the part Ab,
there first occurs the primary crystallization of A. With sinking temperature, the composition of the melt approaches b. When it reaches this point
the montectic three-phase reaction $s_1 + s_2 + A$ sets in, but is interrupted by
the invariant four-phase reaction as soon as the two liquids reach the
respective concentrations i and j. Continued freezing eventually brings
on the stage of binary eutectic crystallization of A and C. Hence, over
this composition range (that is, Ab) there are met successively the three
areas $s_1 + A$, $s_1 + s_2 + A$, and $s_2 + A + C$ (Fig. 109) separated from each other
by isothermal lines. In this connection it should be remembered that the
adjacence of the last two regions is only apparent. Actually they are
separated from each other by the invariant four-phase system. In the

interval *be* the primary precipitation of A occurs from the mixture of two liquid phases. Over *eg* the first evidence of freezing is the solidification of C from the same mixture. The curve *eg* (Fig. 109) is the trace of the front surface, *jmie*, of Fig. 105 upon the vertical plane *Ah*, the point *g* corresponding to the place where the plane crosses the rib *jmi*; *go* represents the cut made by plane *Ah* with the partial surface *jC′Cm*, which is turned away from the observer in Fig. 105. From this figure it is evident that the lower boundary of the field $s_1 + s_2 + C$ must be an isothermal straight line, a fact which is required by the existence of the invariant equilibrium at the close of this reaction. The precipitation of C from homogeneous melt is the first event in the interval *gh*. In the interval *go* (Fig. 103), the path of the melt encounters the line *gj*, and hence a monotectic reaction involving s_1, s_2, and C occurs. On the other hand, the alloys of *oh* are uninfluenced by the region of the two immiscible liquids.

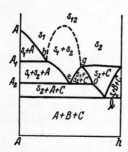

FIG. 109. Section *Ah* (Fig. 103).

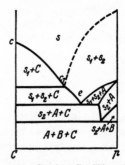

FIG. 110. Section *Cp* (Fig. 103).

Let us next consider the section *Cp* (Fig. 103) which is exhibited in Fig. 110. Over the interval *Ce*, primary crystallization of C occurs first: over Cc_1, from a homogeneous liquid; and in the interval c_1e, from a mixture of two liquids, as shown in Fig. 110. From *e* to *p*, A is the first solid constituent to be precipitated from the liquids s_1 and s_2. The upper and lower boundaries of the region $s_1 + s_2 + C$ must be isothermal lines, since on the boundary surface of this space (Fig. 105) all lines passing through C are conodes.

A section which passes through *p* and to one side of but near C will have a diagram similar to that shown in Fig. 110. The most important difference will be that the region $s_1 + s_2 + C$ will not extend to the side of the section, as will be quite readily understood from studying Fig. 105. In this case, the region $s_1 + s_2 + C$ will have a form somewhat like it has in Fig. 109.

The reader may be left the problem of working out the cases where the vertical plane cuts the three-phase spaces $s_1 + s_2 + A$ or $s_1 + s_2 + C$, but not the space of two liquids. It will be found that the three-phase regions having two molten phases will be involved only temporarily during the freezing process.

D. Additional Cases with a Solubility Gap in the Liquid State

It is evident that the fundamental possibilities for the case of a mechanical mixture with eutectic and the formation of two phases in the liquid state are exhausted. Just as it is impossible in a binary system for the eutectic to occur in an interval of two liquids, so for a ternary system it is impossible that the ternary eutectic shall fall in the region of two immiscible liquids. If this should occur, there would exist simultaneously the five phases s_1, s_2, A, B, and C, a condition contradictory to the phase rule. On the other hand, there is the possibility that three liquid phases could exist in a ternary system. This case will not be taken up since it has not been known actually to occur. Likewise, no consideration will be given to other constitutional cases involving two liquids, such as systems in which solid solutions or compounds occur in the solid state, since these present nothing fundamentally new. In this volume, only the fundamental problems can be presented.

Chapter VIII

Two Binary Systems Form Unbroken Series of Solid Solutions, the Third Has a Gap in Miscibility in the Solid State

1. GENERAL. PROCESS OF CRYSTALLIZATION. STATE SPACES

In the constitutional problem now being set forth, it will be observed that results found in Chapter VII for the liquid state may, under certain conditions, be applied to solid alloys.

In Fig. 111 the constitutional diagram is shown with the binary systems laid down about the concentration triangle. Systems AC and BC form an unbroken series of solid solutions without maxima or minima, but in the third system, AB, there is a gap in solubility and a eutectic point. In the liquid state all three components are mutually completely soluble.

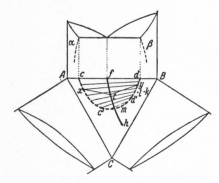

FIG. 111.

The triangle of concentrations in the case of a miscibility gap in the solid state in one binary system and complete miscibility in the liquid state.

The points c and d specify the limits of the interval of insolubility at the temperature of the eutectic point in the system AB. This gap extends in some manner into the ternary system. It cannot, however, reach the other binary systems, since these possess unrestricted solubility in the solid state. Hence, it must end within the ternary system. Such a situation can exist only if the two branches, cc' and dd', extending out from c and d meet in some point, m. In such an event the compositions indicated by the two branches must obviously become identical. Since the two crystalline solids α and β separated by the gap thus become joined together, these two phases must be the same at the point m. Therefore, the point m is a critical point in the sense employed in the previous chapter.

The formal theory concerning heterogeneous equilibria is not concerned about the molecular state of substances, but deals with the crystalline state just as with the liquid or gaseous. Therefore the hypothesis of a critical point in the solid state may be treated in exactly the same way as was done in the previous chapter when discussing regions of insolubility and critical phenomena. However, it is desirable to mention briefly the possibility of such a critical point from the viewpoint of structure.

An isotropic phase, whether a liquid or a gas, is defined by its volume, pressure, temperature, and composition. No more facts are necessary; hence, two liquids which possess the same pressure, temperature, and composition and also necessarily the same volume, are identical. A different situation exists with respect to the crystalline state. For solid substances there is added to the variables of an isotropic phase, a new characteristic —namely, the degree and character of their anisotropy. A crystal may be regular or hexagonal, and in the latter case may have different axial ratios. This new factor is not a true independent variable from the viewpoint of phase theory; it cannot be varied, because each crystal possesses a definite and characteristic state of anisotropy. However, there is the consequence that two crystals of the same volume and the same composition but with different crystal forms may appear to be unlike substances. The experiments of G. Tammann on the application of pressure showed many instances of two crystal forms of one substance existing beside each other at the temperature of transformation and although their volumes were identical, they had decidedly different properties.

In view of these facts, it does not follow at once that if two crystals α and β have the same composition as they do at point m (Fig. 111) they are identical. It is more logical to inquire under what conditions such an assumption can be made.

Obviously these conditions must be similar to those necessary for the formation of an unbroken series of solid solutions between two crystalline substances. Experience has shown that one requirement is that the space lattices of the two components must be the same (within small differences of atomic distance). That this condition is necessary but not sufficient to insure uninterrupted miscibility is also known.

If the metal C forms solid solutions without restriction with both A and B, the space lattices of both A and B must be similar to that of C, and hence to each other. Obviously, this hypothesis is satisfied in the diagram of Fig. 111. Since the space lattices of α and β become continuously more nearly alike, the crystals differ only in composition and become actually identical in m. Therefore m is a critical point.

The above analysis has yielded a concise picture of the constitution of the alloys in the crystalline state. The diagram exhibits a break in solubility, *cmd*, of which the boundary, in general, changes with temperature and which has fundamentally the same nature as a region of immiscibility in the liquid state. It can also happen, in contrast with the situation presented in Fig. 111, that the gap in solubility is entirely within the solid state and is closed above by a critical point. In this case, the system AB also freezes as an unbroken series of solid solutions. Corresponding to each temperature there is a point, m, in which the two phases present in the gap become identical. These points may therefore be termed "partial critical points" and the continuum of all of them described as a "critical curve" as mentioned in Chapter VII. Concerning all these situations there is nothing to be said beyond the analysis given in the previous chapter.

Let us next consider the solidification process in some detail. If the break in solubility, cmd, extends from low temperature up to the freezing point, then during crystallization a three-phase equilibrium will develop in certain concentration areas. The melt and the two crystal forms, α and β, will participate in this equilibrium, which may be considered analogous to the monotectic state space discussed in the previous chapter, except that in the latter there were two liquids and one crystalline substance. The three phases will lie at the corners of conode triangles, as illustrated by xyt in Fig. 111. If the curves cxc' and dyd' slope away from c and d to lower temperatures, then, as seen from C, the point t, representing the melt, must lie in front of the conode xy connecting the two crystalline constituents. In Fig. 111, this assumption regarding the downward slope of cxc' and dyd' has been made. The continuum of compositions of melts which participate in the three-phase equilibrium is represented by the curve fh. The position and nature of its end point, h, will be the subject of later discussion.

The freezing of the alloys having compositions outside the solubility gap proceeds, with one exception which will soon be explained, in exactly the same manner as in a system having complete solubility in the solid state. For example, suppose the alloy, l, begins to freeze in such a way that a solid solution of composition k is precipitated. The compositions of both phases then follow along their respective curves in the way depicted in Chapter III and the molten material is exhausted before its path intercepts the line fh and, accordingly, before the requirements for the formation of a three-phase equilibrium are satisfied. If the melt should reach the curve fh, then the solid metal precipitated would necessarily have a composition on the curve $dd'c'c$. This situation would be impossible, because the average composition of the two phases which compose the alloy must lie on the conode connecting them. Therefore, the discussion of the freezing process may be limited at first to the alloys which lie inside the miscibility gap $cc'md'd$.

The freezing of the alloys of this region occurs in the same manner as for the compositions described in Chapter V which fall in the miscibility gap. After the primary crystallization has been completed, the melt enters the three-phase region in which two kinds of crystals are precipitated. The three-phase triangle shown in Fig. 111 is displaced to lower temperatures until the conode connecting the two solid phases reaches the point representing the composition of the alloy. Solidification is then complete.

Some of the conode triangles (of the type xty), more exactly, those for which the concentration of the melt lies near point h, project beyond the region $cc'd'd$. Fig. 112 shows such triangles on a large scale. One of the corners of these triangles lies on the curve of the eutectic melt fh, while the other two are on the curve $c'md'$ on opposite sides of the critical point m. The envelope of the two sides of the triangles whose apices lie on fh constitutes the surface $c'md'nhoc'$.

The alloys which lie inside this region constitute the exception mentioned above. Regardless of the fact that they lie outside the hetero-

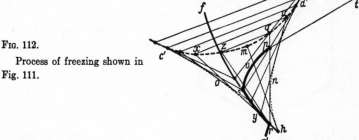

Fig. 112.

Process of freezing shown in Fig. 111.

geneous region, they experience during their freezing an interval in which they break up into three phases, as shown by the following analysis.

Let us consider an alloy of the composition p. It will begin to solidify by precipitating solid solution of some composition t. During further solidification the melt and the solid solution will follow paths whose corresponding points are connected by conodes passing through p. This situation continues only so long as the alloy consists of two phases. The two lines $d's$ and qr, which pass through p, are conodes. Hence, during freezing, the alloy p at some temperature, T_1, consists of the liquid s and the crystalline d', while at some lower temperature, T_2, it is composed of solid solution of composition q and melt of composition r. The second temperature, T_2, must be lower than T_1, since the temperature decreases in passing along the curve $d'qm$ from d' toward m. During solidification of the alloy, the composition of the solid solution moves along the curve td' from t toward d', while simultaneously the composition of the melt follows the curve pvs. When the points d' and s, respectively, are reached, the precipitation of a second solid solution begins. The alloy then enters the three-phase region, the point p, moving into the conode triangle of the three-phase region. An example of such a triangle is uyx. As the temperature drops, the compositions of the crystalline phases follow along the curves $d'uq$ and $c'xz$, while the composition of the melt moves along syr. The amount of the second crystal type, which lies on the curve $c'xz$, first increases and then decreases, and finally becomes zero as the composition reaches z, since at this point, the alloy p again consists of only two phases, q and r. Thus, the three-phase region is left behind and further solidification proceeds as in the simple case of homogeneous solid solutions; the composition of the melt continues along some curve, rr', while that of the solid solution starts from q and finishes at p. The final result of the freezing process is a homogeneous solid solution, p.

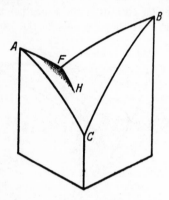

Fig. 113.

Space diagram corresponding to Fig. 111.

Fig. 113 shows the space diagram for the case under consideration. The trough in the liquidus surface becomes flatter in going from F toward H, and disappears at the latter point. Below H the liquidus surface is continuous.

That part of the space of binary eutectic crystallization which relates to alloys lying within the heterogeneous region $cc'd'd$ (Fig. 111) has exactly the same form as the one considered in Chapter V. It is a three-edged space which extends inward from a conode on the side AB and becomes rapidly narrower as it approaches the point m. The upper boundary of the region is formed by the movement of two conodes which intersect each other on the curve fh of doubly saturated liquid. The lower boundary is formed by the downward gliding of the line which ties together the corresponding points cd, xy, etc. For alloys within the curve $cc'd'd$, the lower boundary surface is reached before the melt attains the composition h.[*]

---

[*] Note by translator: The original has m instead of the h used in this translation. The melt does not at any time have the composition m and certainly not all the alloys of the region of immiscibility become solidified (reach the bottom surface) before the composition of the melt extends beyond the boundary $cc'd'd$ (or $cc'md'd$ for consistency with previous methods of specifying such regions).

The situation is quite different for those alloys outside the heterogeneous region in which, temporarily, three phases are formed. On the upper surface of the ternary state space the rib *fh* is still to be found. The lower boundary has transformed into a curved surface. The form of the entire three-phase space is difficult to represent by a sketch. It can be understood more satisfactorily from the sections shortly to be described.

2. Isothermal Sections

The isothermal sections above the region of binary eutectic crystallization reveal nothing in addition to facts brought out in previous cases. An isothermal section (Fig. 114) at about the temperature of the eutectic curve *fh* is of interest. As the temperature decreases, the three-phase triangle existing in the successive sections becomes narrower until, upon

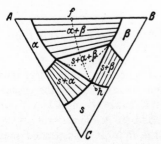

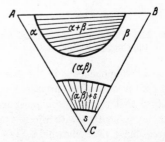

Fig. 114. Isothermal section in the temperature range of binary eutectic crystallization (Figs. 111-113).

Fig. 115. Isothermal section of the system shown in Fig. 114 after conclusion of the eutectic crystallization.

reaching the temperature of the point *h*, it has shrunk to the conode *mh*. At the same time the boundary curves of the area of the melt against the regions *s+α* and *s+β* gradually undergo a realignment and at the temperature *h* meet to form a continuous curve. For temperatures slightly below *h*, the various areas are the two-phase portion *α+β*, the band of homogeneous solid (*α, β*) solution, the two-phase field of melt and solid (*α, β*) solution, and finally, adjoining the component *C*, the single-phase field of the liquid alloy (Fig. 115).

3. Vertical Sections

Of special interest among the vertical sections are those which intersect the part of the three-phase space which lies outside of the heterogeneous region; in other words, those which pass between the points *m* and *h*. The cuts *op*, *qr*, *vu*, and *wu* will be examined (Fig. 116). The section *op* is represented schematically in Fig. 117. It is similar to one of the examples given in Chapter V and requires no explanation. It may be noted, how-

ever, that the intersection point o_1 with the three-phase space lies at a
temperature higher than point p_1, in agreement with the positions of the
conodes in Fig. 111.

In the section qr the curve fh of doubly saturated melt still produces a
crease in the liquidus surface; hence, there is a kink, q_1, in the corresponding curve in Fig. 118. On the other hand, all the alloys of this sec-

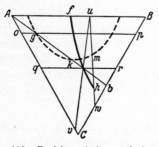

FIG. 116. Position of the vertical sections op, qr, wu, vu, and Ab.

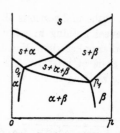

FIG. 117. Section op (Fig. 116).

tion are homogeneous in the solid state, and hence the solidus curve must
be continuous. This apparent contradiction is explained by the circumstance that the three-phase space in the interval between m and h does
not make contact with the region of the solid state. The section of the
three-phase field shown in Fig. 118 has the form of a suspended sack.
This sack-shaped field must have a continuous lower boundary since the

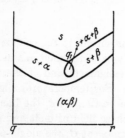

FIG. 118. Section qr (Fig. 116).

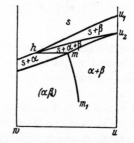

FIG. 119. Section wu (Fig. 116).

crystalline phases in the adjoining field comprise an unbroken series of
solid solutions which, however, vary in composition from α to β.

The cut wu goes through the points h and m which lie on a conode and
are, accordingly, at the same temperature. In this cut the liquidus curve
is of the continuous type, because at the point h the crease outlined by the
curve fh has been flattened (Fig. 119). Over the interval u_1h, β solid solution is first precipitated, and this process is followed by the binary eutectic

crystallization of α and β, as shown in the triangle hmu_2 of Fig. 119. After cooling through this three-phase region, the alloys next enter a two-phase area, either $\alpha+\beta$ or melt$+\alpha$. Characterizing the solid solution precipitated below the three-phase space of α and especially contrasting it with β is quite arbitrary, since m is a point on the critical curve lying on the boundary surface separating the region of one solid solution from the space of the mixture of two solid solutions. On this curve the crystalline phases are identical. In general, the curve mm_1 (Fig. 119) does not coincide with the critical curve and hence a choice between the forms α and β may be made. However, if mm_1 does coincide with the critical curve, which is a possible case, such a differentiation is impossible. The critical separation curve mm_1 then indicates, in this special case only, that to the left of it the two substances α and β have become identical in character. For this reason, in Fig. 119 this field has been marked $(\alpha\beta)$ instead of simply α.

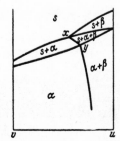

FIG. 120. Section vu (Fig. 116).

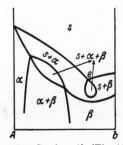

FIG. 121. Section Ab (Fig. 116).

The cut vu (Fig. 120) is quite similar to that shown in Fig. 119. The three-phase field is no longer separated from the $s+\alpha$ region by a horizontal line, since the three-phase space is cut slantingly by the plane vu. The intersection, x, of the vertical plane with the curve fh must lie at a higher temperature than its intersection, y, with the curve $cc'd'd$, for the latter lies inside the isothermal conode triangle associated with x.

Section Ab (Fig. 121) has a special form which arises from the condition that it cuts the three-phase space twice, as is quite possible: first, in the interval gk and again in the vicinity of the curve fh (Fig. 116). This situation exists because the three-phase space lies partly outside $cc'd'd$ and has an arrow-like projection extending toward h. The liquidus line of this section shows a discontinuity at the intersection with fh; to the left of the discontinuity is the region of primary crystallization of α, and to its right the region in which β is first precipitated. At the discontinuity, e, a three-phase region is joined on in the manner already shown in Fig. 118. The areas of primary solidification of α and β completely surround the small three-phase area. After completion of the primary crystallization of α, the alloys of the interval gk enter the region of binary eutectic solidification of α and β. The plane Ab cuts only two sides of the conode triangle which generates the ternary space—namely, the side which connects the melt with the α crystals and the side which connects the α and β solid solutions. At no point does it make contact with the third side, which ties together the melt with the associated β substance. Hence the left-hand three-phase region has only two boundary curves, as shown in Fig. 121. Just below this field is found the two-phase area of α and β solid solutions.

The circumstance of a plane intersecting a state space twice presents no peculiar difficulties and may appear in other instances—for example, if the boundary surface of a state space has a complicated or folded form. Such forms are readily possible, though they were not postulated in the constitutional case which has been described. In the instance given above, the double intersection arose from the special form of the state space.

Chapter IX

Iron-Silicon-Aluminum Alloys

1. INTRODUCTION

The alloys of aluminum are of special interest among alloy systems of
ternary and higher degree not only because the most valuable alloys are
prepared by the addition of two or more metals, as exemplified by Dur-
alumin with 3 to 4 per cent copper, 0.5 per cent magnesium, and 0.5 per
cent manganese, or Lautal with 3 to 4 per cent copper, 1 to 2 per cent
silicon, and 0 to 1 per cent manganese, but because commercial aluminum
practically always contains impurities, particularly iron and silicon. Industrial aluminum and its alloys are always systems of three or more
components; hence, a knowledge of ternary systems is important in their

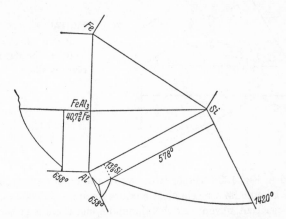

FIG. 122. Triangle of concentrations of the aluminum-silicon-
iron alloys.

theoretical treatment. Furthermore, the impurities in industrial aluminum have a considerable influence on the mechanical behavior of the
metal, so that for many purposes their presence cannot be neglected.

In general, the alloys of aluminum are characterized by only a limited
solid solubility of aluminum for other components but the metal is much
inclined to the formation of compounds. The ternary systems are very
complicated for this reason and a complete analysis of them is most
difficult. However, since only the aluminum-rich alloys are important, it

is permissible to limit the discussion to the aluminum corner. In the present chapter, only the description of the iron-silicon-aluminum system will be given. This system is involved in all industrial alloys and has a special importance for this reason.

2. Process of Crystallization. State Spaces

In spite of much careful study, the ternary system of the iron-silicon-aluminum alloys has not yet been completely explained, even in the aluminum corner. Noticeable contradictions exist between the results of the various investigators. This condition is partly due to failure to obtain a true equilibrium state because of the sluggishness of the alloys. Hence, the ternary system given here has only a tentative character.

The results to be shown are based on the work of Fuss[2] and some accounts in English.[3] The concentration triangle of the ternary alloys is

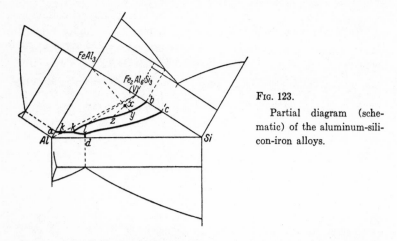

Fig. 123.

Partial diagram (schematic) of the aluminum-silicon-iron alloys.

reproduced in Fig. 122 together with two of the binary systems. Silicon forms with aluminum a mechanical mixture having a eutectic at approximately 13 per cent silicon. At the aluminum end there is at the completion of freezing a solid solution containing about 1.6 per cent silicon, but as the temperature falls the percentage of silicon in solution decreases rapidly. However, the present discussion will not be concerned with changes in the solid state but will be limited to the solidification process.

Formation of an aluminum-rich solid solution in the iron-aluminum system to any appreciable extent has not been demonstrated. In the following analysis a very low solubility of iron in aluminum will be assumed.

Aluminum forms a number of compounds with iron, of which the one richest in aluminum has the formula $FeAl_3$. In Fig. 122, the system is exhibited as possessing a small open maximum as reported by Gwyer and Phillips.[4] Actually the maximum may be a covered one.[5] The situation appears to be a border-line case, and since the behavior at the aluminum corner would not be materially affected, the assumption of an open maximum will be retained. The form of the iron-aluminum diagram at higher concentrations of iron and that of the iron-silicon system are of little interest in considering the aluminum-rich alloys.

The outlines of the assumed constitution as set down by Fuss are as follows:

(1) The section $FeAl_3$-Si is quasi-binary (see Chapter IV). This circumstance permits us to restrict the study to the partial triangle Al-$FeAl_3$-Si.

(2) In this quasi-binary section there is a ternary compound $Fe_2Al_6Si_3$, which crystallizes peritectically with a covered maximum.

As a basis for further discussion, it will be convenient to use the partial concentration triangle $FeAl_3$-Si-Al, shown with its associated binary systems in Fig. 123. As will be observed from the diagram, the system forms practically no solid solutions and has on one side a compound which originates in a peritectic reaction. This case has not been explained in every detail but with the aid of the analyses of Chapters IV and V its treatment offers no difficulty.

From the invariant points a, b, c, and d of the binary systems, there must extend out into the ternary system curves of doubly saturated liquid. From a, c, and d these curves will be of the binary eutectic type, while from b a binary peritectic curve will originate. These curves must intersect somehow in the interior of the ternary system, and their intersection points will correspond to invariant equilibria of the liquid with three crystalline phases. It may be easily shown that the two curves, bk and cl, cannot meet; if they should, a contradiction would arise like that demonstrated in Chapter IV, section C, since here also three crystalline phases $FeAl_3$, $Fe_2Al_6Si_3$, and Si lie in a quasi-binary system on one straight line in the concentration triangle. Accordingly, there is only one possibility—namely, that the curve bk of the peritectic reaction

$$\text{melt } s + FeAl_3 \rightleftarrows Fe_2Al_6Si_3 \tag{1}$$

encounters the eutectic curve ak of the eutectic reaction

$$\text{melt } s \rightleftarrows FeAl_3 + Al. \tag{2}$$

When the melt has attained the composition k, the following phases exist simultaneously in invariant equilibrium: melt, Al, $FeAl_3$, and $Fe_2Al_6Si_3$. Since k lies outside the triangle formed by these three solid phases, it must be a ternary peritectic point. If it lay to the left of the line Al-$Fe_2Al_6Si_3$—for example, in the position k'—it would correspond to a ternary eutectic point. Such a position is theoretically possible and could occur in a way similar to that described in Chapter IV, section B, illustrating the transition of a binary eutectic into a ternary peritectic, except that the transformation would proceed in the reverse manner. The exact location of k is not known, but for simplicity it will be assumed to have a peritectic position.

The peritectic reaction experienced by the melt of composition k is, if the ternary compound $Fe_2Al_6Si_3$ is designated by V,

$$s + FeAl_3 \rightleftharpoons Al + V. \tag{3}$$

For the present, the existence of the small region of solid solution adjacent to the aluminum corner will be ignored.

In those alloys which have compositions within the triangle Al-FeAl$_3$-V, assuming no relatively insoluble envelopes surround the precipitated grains, the melt will be consumed in the peritectic reaction. Hence, freezing is completed at k by the reaction (3). On the other hand, if the com-

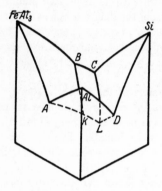

Fig. 124.

·Space diagram corresponding to Fig. 123.

position of the alloy lies outside this triangle and no envelopes have formed about the grains, the compound FeAl$_3$ will be exhausted first. In this event, the freezing alloy will reach a three-phase equilibrium, $s + Al + V$. The melt of this equilibrium lies on the curve kl. Its temperature decreases in going from k to l. At the point l there occurs the ternary eutectic crystallization of the phases Al, V, and Si for all alloys of the partial triangle Al-V-Si.

Fig. 124 shows schematically the prism of state with its liquidus surface. Over the surface FeAl$_3$-B-K-A-FeAl$_3$, FeAl$_3$ is precipitated until the melt, moving along the conode which extends out from the corner FeAl$_3$, reaches one of the curves BK or AK. Depending upon which curve the melt reaches, there occurs either the binary peritectic reaction (1) or the eutectic reaction (2). In systems having a binary compound with an open maximum (Chapter IV) completion of the three-phase reaction is always followed directly by the ternary invariant four-phase conversion. In the present case, an interesting exception occurs for those alloys lying in the portion $VbkV$ (Fig. 123) because the compound FeAl$_3$ is used up during the binary peritectic reaction before the melt reaches the point k. As an example, consider the alloy x. During the primary crystallization of FeAl$_3$ the composition of the melt is displaced to point y, whereupon the peritectic reaction sets in and the composition of the liquid moves along the curve bk toward k. The alloy can consist of three phases—melt, FeAl$_3$, and V—only as long as the point x lies within the triangle formed by the compositions of these three phases. Obviously this condition will cease to exist as soon as the melt reaches the composition z on line Vxz. The alloy then consists of only z and V, the phase FeAl$_3$ having been consumed. From this point, primary crystallization of V occurs until the melt reaches a composition on cl or kl, after which further solidification proceeds in the

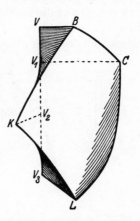

Fig. 125.

State space of primary crystallization of the compound V (Fig. 123).

manner normal for a mechanical mixture, until the eutectic point l is attained. In the region $bklc$ the precipitation of V occurs first; in region (Si)cld, Si is crystallized initially; and in (Al)ald, primary crystals of Al are formed first. The whole process of solidification for these regions does not differ from the manner followed by the mechanical mixtures considered in Chapter II.

Let us consider next the state spaces which arise upon solidification. The space of primary crystallization of FeAl$_3$ has exactly the same form as the space shown in Fig. 11 (p. 20), for a mechanical mixture. The space of primary solidification of the peritectically crystallizing V is exhibited in Fig. 125. $BCLK$ is the liquidus surface which indicates the compositions of the melt saturated in V. Naturally, the amount of V for alloys on this surface is infinitely small. Besides this area, the state space has the additional upper boundary surface indicated by $VBKV_2$. This is the boundary against the region of the binary peritectic crystallization which produces V from the reaction of melt and FeAl$_3$. Typical of the boundary against a three-phase space, this surface is generated through the gliding of a conode one end of which passes through V and the other moves along BK. As we have seen, the complete upper boundary surface signifies that the region of primary crystallization of V can be reached, as the temperature decreases, not only directly from the melt but also after passing through a binary peritectic reaction. The lower boundary of this space is typical of a space of primary crystallization—that is, it consists of two screw-shaped surfaces of which one (V_1CLV_3) separates the space under consideration from the region of the binary eutectic crystallization of V and Si, and the other (V_2KLV_3) separates it from the similar region of V and Al. The first is not visible at all in Fig. 125, and the second only partly so.

There is yet to be discussed the three-phase space of binary peritectic solidification. It must have the form of a three-cornered tube; its surfaces are generated by conodes which glide along curves representing the com-

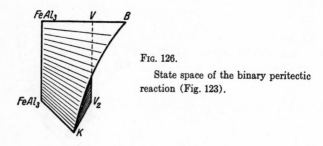

Fig. 126.

State space of the binary peritectic reaction (Fig. 123).

positions of the phases contributing to the three-phase equilibrium. The first of these conodes connects FeAl$_3$ with the melt, the second connects V with the melt, and the third, FeAl$_3$ with V. When intersected by an isothermal plane, this three-phase space reveals the conode triangle so frequently encountered. The space under discussion is shown in Fig. 126. The only way in which it differs from the space of binary eutectic crystallization shown in Fig. 12 (p. 22) is that in the latter case, both kinds of precipitated crystals lie at the ends of a vertical sequence of conodes from which the state space extended, whereas in the present figure, the melt lies at one end of the corresponding conode. The result of this arrangement is that the rib produced as the ternary space reaches out into the interior of the prism of state extends out from B. Furthermore, the surface which is developed by the gliding of the conode VB lies on the sloping underside of the state space. This surface is the same as shown by the corresponding letters $VBKV_2$ in Fig. 125 and separates the three-phase space from the region of primary crystallization of V which exists at lower temperatures.

A consideration of the remaining state spaces may be omitted, since they offer nothing in advance of examples given in Chapters II and IV, as the reader may easily convince himself.

3. CRYSTALLINE STATE

We next pass to the discussion of the crystalline state. Of greatest interest is the small region of solid solution in the aluminum corner. Fig. 127 represents a schematic section after the completion of solidification.

Adjoining the field of the aluminum-rich solid solution are the two-phase regions $\alpha + FeAl_3$ and $\alpha + V$. The position of the point d on the side Al-Si of the concentration triangle is in agreement with the assumption that the α solid solution, which is in equilibrium with silicon, is free from iron. If iron were present, the point d would not lie on the side Al-Si but would be some distance—perhaps a short one—inside the concentration triangle. Such a situation would mean that between d and the side there existed still another two-phase region, $\alpha + Si$.

The position of the point b is not known exactly; however, the following statements may be made. The solubility of silicon in solid aluminum is

FIG. 127.

Partial diagram of the aluminum-silicon-iron alloys section in the solid state.

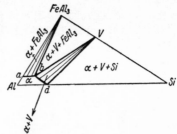

known to be very much dependent on temperature. At low temperatures, the point d is very close to the aluminum corner. If the α solid solution existing in equilibrium with the compound V contained appreciable amounts of silicon—meaning that b must lie close to d—one would expect that after suitable heat treatment of a mixture of α solid solution and compound V, there would be a precipitation of Si crystals. However, Fuss was not able to bring out such a structural change in a mixture of this type, which fact would indicate that the point b must lie in the immediate neighborhood of a, hence quite near the aluminum corner. Unfortunately, the location of this point is not easy to determine, since the compound, V, is developed peritectically and is therefore inclined to form a covering around the previously precipitated crystals of FeAl₃. Hence, the possibility still exists that b coincides with d; Fuss himself appeared to favor this idea. (It must be remarked that the statements of Fuss in the previously cited work are very brief and occasionally unintelligible. His illustrations of the concentration triangles are not free from confusion.)

Gwyer and Phillips have stated that three ternary compounds are formed within the ternary system Al-Fe-Si. As has been mentioned, this question has not been definitely settled. In this discussion we have used the diagram worked out by Fuss because his work is later and the results simpler. Furthermore, only one compound has been revealed by x-ray investigations.

In consideration of the fact that V always forms around the compound $FeAl_3$, the presence of the latter substance during the primary crystallization of V must always be reckoned with throughout the region bounded by $akzb$ (Fig. 123). This condition may appear in industrial alloys when the iron content is higher than corresponds to the eutectic point a—that is, above about 2 per cent. In the partial region $bklc$ there occurs, as has been previously mentioned, the primary solidification of V, and in the field (Si) cld, of Si. Both types of primary crystal formation may occur in Silumin, which is an alloy containing about 13 per cent silicon, or the eutectic proportion (point d). If the Silumin becomes contaminated with iron, as may happen during manufacturing when iron-containing aluminum is frequently used, the composition will move away from the point d into the interior of the system. If sufficient iron is introduced, the composition of the alloy may pass beyond the lines kl or lc.

Chapter X

Tin-Zinc-Copper Alloys

1. BINARY SYSTEMS

Of the many important ternary systems based on copper, only the copper-zinc-tin alloys will be examined. The description of this system, which is the basis of the red brasses, follows closely the investigations of Tammann and Hansen.[6] Both of the binary systems zinc-copper and tin-copper exhibit very complicated diagrams and, as would be expected, the ternary system is likewise complex. The present discussion will be limited to the copper-rich portion as worked out by the above authors. This portion is also the region of the industrially important alloys.

FIG. 128.

Partial diagram of the tin-copper alloys, according to M. Hamasumi and S. Nishigara.

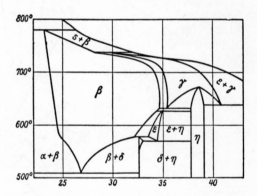

A difficulty in describing this system arises immediately from the fact that the copper-tin system has not been worked out in the same satisfactory manner as the constitution of the copper-zinc alloys. The constitutional diagram developed by Bauer and Vollenbruck[7] and used by Tammann and Hansen is questionable in some details. In the following analysis we shall use the recently published results of M. Hamasumi and S. Nishigori,[8] although their diagram should not be considered as final. The part of this diagram which is of interest to us is presented in Fig. 128. Inspection shows that three crystalline types α, β, and γ are precipitated from the copper-rich melt. During cooling, the γ substance breaks up into other crystal forms, but on account of the complexity of the system there is some uncertainty regarding the exact arrangement. The ϵ and η forms are without technical significance. A transformation of the β crystals also occurs upon cooling. In this case the products are the α and δ crystals (the ϵ substance being disregarded). The δ phase is classed among the industrially important types since it occurs in many engineering alloys. The pursuit of the transformations of the γ, ϵ, η, and δ crystalline forms

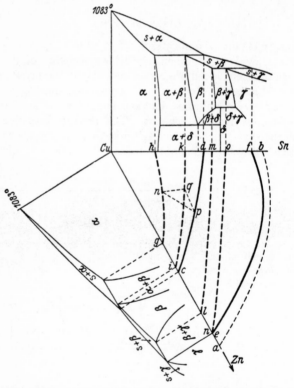

FIG. 129. The copper corner of the triangle of concentrations of tin-zinc-copper alloys. (See note, page 142).

into the ternary system would be difficult and of little profit since many of these changes have not been satisfactorily explained. Under the circumstances, it is desirable to use for the tin-copper system a schematic and simplified constitutional diagram from which consideration of the ϵ phase is omitted. This simplified diagram and that of the copper-zinc ternary diagram are shown in full lines and the solidus in dotted ones. Corresponding to the practice in this book, the liquidus curves within the alloys are shown in Fig. 129 laid out on the sides of the ternary triangle.

According to this simplified scheme, β and γ combine in a eutectoidal* reaction to form δ substance. Upon further cooling to about 520° C the β material breaks up eutectoidally into α and δ crystals.

In the binary system copper-zinc, three kinds of crystals, α, β, and γ, are precipitated from the melt. Thus, the behavior of this system is similar to that of the tin-copper, but is considerably simpler in the part which is of interest in our discussion, particularly because both the β and γ forms are stable down to ordinary temperatures. A transformation occurring in the β substance will be neglected.

Consideration of the binary system tin-zinc may be omitted since only the copper-rich portion is being examined.

2. PROCESS OF CRYSTALLIZATION. STATE SPACES

In the following discussion we shall restrict ourselves to that part of the ternary diagram in which α, β, or γ substances are precipitated as primary crystals—that is, the part inside the line ab in Fig. 129.

The α solid solutions formed along the tin and zinc sides of the diagram both have the same crystal form, as is obvious since both adjoin the copper corner. Also the β phases in the two binary systems are isomorphous and possess an unlimited mutual solubility, so that immediately after solidification there is a band-like continuous space of homogeneous β substance extending through the ternary system from the zinc to the tin side. The same condition seems to be true for the γ crystals, but this point has not been thoroughly investigated. We shall assume that the γ solid solutions on the copper-tin side and on the copper-zinc side are isomorphous and completely soluble in each other.

Freezing proceeds exactly as described in Chapter V, section B. The liquidus surface which separates the region of homogeneous melt from the regions of two-phase spaces of primary precipitation consists of three parts: part (Cu) cd in which the primary crystallization of α substance occurs, part $cdfe$ in which β crystals first appear, and the part beyond ef, with whose outer boundary we are not concerned and in which primary solidification of γ crystals takes place. This surface appears as shown in Fig. 130 when looked at across the concentration triangle toward the copper corner. The different parts are labeled to correspond to the type of substance which precipitates first. The capital letters correspond to the lower case ones of Fig. 129.

The melts which lie on the line cd are in equilibrium simultaneously with both α and β crystals of which the compositions lie on the curves gh and ik (Fig. 129), respectively. These three phases create a three-cornered

---

* Note by translator: The statement that this reaction is eutectoidal appears strange, as the diagram indicates a peritectoidal reaction. In a eutectic reaction, one substance breaks up into two. In the present case, two substances combine to form one, a type of reaction which is ordinarily called "peritectic." However, Masing continues to call this transformation "eutectoidal."

tube of binary peritectic crystallization of the form described in Chapter V. An isothermal section of this space is illustrated by the triangle nqp* in Fig. 129. Some idea of the shape may be gained from observing that the temperature of the equilibrium curves decreases in passing from the

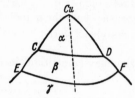

FIG. 130.

Liquidus surface of the tin-zinc-copper alloys at the copper corner.

zinc side to the tin side. Quite similar behavior occurs for the melts *ef* (Fig. 129) which are in equilibrium with both the β phase along *lm* and the γ substance along *no*.

In the solid state, the crystalline forms α, β, and γ are separated by solubility gaps in which the alloys are composed of two phases. Specifically, these gaps are the two-phase spaces $\alpha+\beta$ and $\beta+\gamma$.

Fig. 131 represents the space of α solid solution when looked at across the prism of state toward the copper edge. The two-phase regions adjoining this space are noted on the various surfaces. $GH(\text{Cu})$ is the

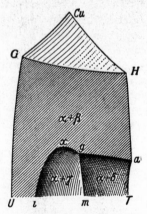

FIG. 131.

State space of α solid solution looked at in the direction toward copper.

solidus surface of the α substance; $UGHa$ outlines the boundary between the α and $\alpha+\beta$ spaces. The nature of this boundary surface at low temperatures will be considered later; for the present, only the portions which are concerned with the freezing of the alloys will be described.

* Note by translator: The triangle nqp in Fig. 129 is incorrectly placed. The point p on cd should lie further from the copper-zinc side than the points n and q. It should also be noticed that the α-β peritectic on the zinc side is actually higher than on the tin side instead of lower as drawn in Fig. 129.

Between the single-phase spaces of the melt and the α solid solution lies
the two-phase region of primary solidification of the latter phase. This
space has the appearance shown in Fig. 132 when seen from a point below
it and near the copper edge. *HGCD* is the boundary surface against the
three-phase space α+β+melt.

The space of β phase is shown in Fig. 133 where the observer is again
looking toward the edge which represents copper. On the back portion,

Fig. 132.

    State space of the primary solidifica-
tion of α substance.

not visible, the β solid solution is in equilibrium with the α substance.
LIKM is the solidus surface. On the forward surface the β phase is in
equilibrium with γ solid solution. The conditions at low temperatures will
be described in section 3 of this chapter.

The homogeneous space of γ phase has the form exhibited in Fig. 136
(when looked at from the copper edge). The lettering corresponds to
that given in Fig. 129. This space will be described in more detail in the
following section.

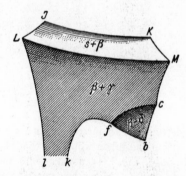

Fig. 133.

    State space of β solid solution when
looked at away from copper.

3. Reactions in the Crystalline State. State Spaces

As has been demonstrated, the process of solidification is very simple.
The difficulty in getting a comprehensive view of the whole system comes
from the numerous transformations which occur in the solid state. These
changes are so complicated that we have already had occasion to simplify
the diagram of the tin-copper alloys for our theoretical discussion. We
shall start out from the tin-copper alloys and attempt gradually to gain
an understanding of the transformations which occur in the solid state.

Such a view can be considered to have only an outline form. The various details are likely to be modified by later experimental work.

According to the above mentioned investigations of Tammann and Hansen, the temperature of the transformation during which the β phase changes into α and δ substances rises in moving away from the tin-copper side into the interior of the ternary system. Nothing definite can be stated concerning the reaction by which the δ phase is produced from β and γ especially since the form shown in Fig. 129 is only hypothetical. Since, however, in the zinc-rich alloys β phase exists beside γ phase at low temperature, the assumption must be made that the temperature of the

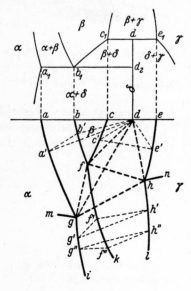

Fig. 134.

Invariant reaction in the tin-rich alloys (peritectic case).

eutectoidal formation of δ substance decreases with increasing zinc content. The simplest course of events within the prism would be that the two three-phase equilibria, β, γ, and δ ($c_1 d_1 e_1$, Fig. 134), during which the last-named phase is formed and α, β, and δ ($a_1 b_1 d_2$), where the β constituent breaks up, should come together inside the ternary system and form an invariant four-phase equilibrium. Such a scheme is depicted in Fig. 134; ae is the tin-copper side of the concentration triangle on which has been erected a part of the tin-copper diagram shown in Fig. 129. The heavy lines lie within the concentration triangle.

The δ crystals form solid solutions over only a very limited range and their solubility may be neglected. Starting out from the eutectoidal equilibrium $\beta + \gamma \rightleftarrows \delta$ (the horizontal $c_1 d_1 e_1$) the three-phase space develops in the interior of the ternary system into the form of a three-cornered tube, dropping away to lower temperature. Although the composition of the δ crystals (point d) remains approximately unchanged, the compositions of the $β$ and $γ$ phases, which participate in this equilibrium, move along the curves cf and eh to lower temperatures. The isothermal sections through the three-edged tube are triangles of the kind illustrated by $c'de'$.

The three-phase line $a_1b_1d_2$, which corresponds to the reaction $β \rightleftarrows α + δ$, is likewise expanded to a three-cornered tube inside the ternary system. The composition of $α$ phase participating in this equilibrium is displaced along the curve ag, that of the $β$ phase along bf, both curves climbing to higher temperature, while the δ substance remains practically unchanged at point d. Isothermal cuts of this state space may be illustrated by the triangle $a'b'd'$.

The $β$ solid solution at f, the point of intersection of the two curves bf and cf, is in equilibrium with three other phases $α$, $γ$, and δ. Hence it takes part in an invariant equilibrium. The other participating phases have compositions corresponding to the following points: $α - g$, $γ - h$, and δ − d. As was pointed out in Chapter I, the four-sided plane figure $dhgf$ corresponds to an invariant reaction which occurs at constant temperature and composition of the reacting phases, but increases the amount of two of them at the expense of the other two. This is the type of reaction which, if a molten phase were present, would be termed "peritectic four-phase." In this case where all the phases are solid, the reaction is called "peritectoid." From the standpoint of phase theory, there is no difference between the peritectic and peritectoid reactions.

In the present instance, it is clear from geometric analysis, that the peritectoid reaction must consist in the conversion of $β$ and $γ$ to $α$ and δ:

$$β_f + γ_h \rightleftarrows α_g + δ_d.$$

The subscripts indicate the compositions of the phases taking part in the equilibrium.

The problem of determining in which direction this reaction will proceed when heat is withdrawn is a very simple one. The plane of the invariant reaction separates two regions from each other; in one, the phases $β$ and $γ$ but not $α$ and δ can coexist, whereas in the other, $α$ and δ but not $β$ and $γ$ can be present simultaneously. Since the three-phase region of $α$, $β$, and δ crystals, as we have seen, reaches the plane of invariant equilibrium as the temperature is increasing; hence, from underneath, it is obvious that $α$ and δ exist beside each other below the invariant equilibrium of $α$, $β$, $γ$, and δ, whereas from analogous considerations regarding the nature of the three-phase space of $β$, $γ$, and δ, $β$ and $γ$ evidently can coexist only at higher temperatures. Therefore, for a withdrawal of heat, the above-stated peritectoidal reaction proceeds from left to right.

Actually, the plane of invariant equilibrium is reached from higher temperature by two three-phase spaces, the space of β, γ, and α phases and the space of β, γ, and δ phases. The second has already been discussed; it extends out from the binary copper-tin system and ends at the four-phase plane quadrilateral. Among the alloys high in zinc it is no longer observed. Conversely, the space of α, β, and γ attains the invariant plane from the zinc-rich portion. The latter space has yet to be considered; its isothermal section near the plane of invariant equilibrium is illustrated by the triangle $g'f'h'$. The joining of the two three-phase triangles $\alpha_g\beta_f\gamma_h$ and $\delta_d\beta_f\gamma_h$ produces the quadrilateral $gfdh$ of invariant equilibrium.

After the continued withdrawal of heat has brought the invariant reaction to a close, either the β or the γ phase will have been used up. In the first case the three remaining phases will be α_g, γ_h, and δ_d; in the second, α_g, β_f, and δ_d. From the two triangles fgd and gdh, the three-phase spaces

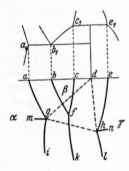

FIG. 135.

System of Fig. 134 on the assumption of a eutectic arrangement.

$\alpha+\beta+\delta$ and $\alpha+\gamma+\delta$ extend to lower temperatures. The first of these has already been examined and found to terminate in the binary tin-copper system on the horizontal line $a_1b_1d_2$. The second progresses toward the zinc-rich alloys. We shall soon concern ourselves with it.

Each of the four phases which participate in the invariant equilibrium takes part in three three-phase equilibria which are connected with the invariant one. For example, the α phase appears in the three systems $\alpha+\beta+\gamma$, $\alpha+\beta+\delta$, and $\alpha+\gamma+\delta$. The sequence of state points of the several phases which participate in these equilibria form cusps on their homogeneous state regions. Hence, for each phase there are three boundary curves which intersect in the composition at which the phase participates in the invariant equilibrium. For the α phase these curves are ag for the equilibrium $\alpha+\beta+\delta$, gi for the equilibrium $\alpha+\beta+\gamma$, and gm for the equilibrium $\alpha+\gamma+\delta$. The assumption has been made that the last curve falls steeply to lower temperatures. The three corresponding curves for the β substance are bf for $\alpha+\beta+\delta$, fc for $\beta+\gamma+\delta$, and fk for $\alpha+\beta+\gamma$; and for the γ solid solution they are eh for $\beta+\gamma+\delta$, hn for $\alpha+\gamma+\delta$, and hl for $\alpha+\beta+\gamma$. The curve hn drops rapidly to low temperatures in much the same manner as *gm*. The crystalline δ constitutes a variation from the general behavior, since its composition is fixed at point *d*, and therefore its state point can move only along a vertical line. Each set of three curves incloses with the associated connecting surfaces a three-edged three-phase region. For example, the curves *gi*, *fk*, and *hl* mark out the three-phase space of α, β, and γ substance; the curves *gm*, *hn*, and the vertical line passing through *d* outline the region of α, γ, and δ crystals; and so on.

The arrangement which would exist under the assumption that a eutectoidal rather than a peritectoidal change occurs is represented in Fig. 135. In the eutectoidal case the β phase could exist only above or

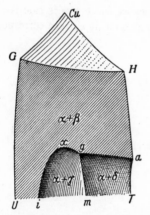

FIG. 131. State space of α solid solution looked at in the direction toward copper.

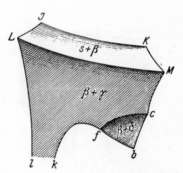

FIG. 133. State space of β solid solution when looked at away from copper.

only below the temperature of invariant equilibrium. Since, however, the temperature of the invariant equilibrium has been found experimentally to lie between b_1 and c_1, the assumption of a eutectoidal change contradicts the experimental facts. For this reason no further attention will be paid to the eutectoidal hypothesis.

On the basis of the above discussion it is now possible to give a more complete description of the low-temperature part of the region of α solid solution as exhibited in Fig. 131. The points labeled with small letters correspond to the points similarly marked in Fig. 134. The point *g* represents a corner of the four-phase quadrilateral. The curves *ga* and *gm* extend out from this point and run to lower temperatures. The curve *gi*, on the other hand, must first rise to higher temperature as the percentage of zinc increases. Its further course is determined by the condition that on the zinc side β phase still exists at ordinary temperature. To satisfy this condition, the curve must pass through a maximum at some point, x, and then descend rapidly, as shown in Fig. 131.

An account can be given also of the region of homogeneous β substance (Fig. 133). Below, this region is bounded by the rib bf along which the β phase is in equilibrium with the α phase on curve ag and with the δ crystals at point d. The point f in Fig. 133 lies at the same temperature as g in Fig. 131. The curve fk, like gi, in moving toward the zinc-rich side must rise to higher temperatures and then drop rather abruptly. The rear surface of Fig. 133, on which the β phase is in equilibrium with the α phase, possesses no complexities at low temperatures. On the front side of the portion cfb, the β substance is in equilibrium with the δ phase.

The space of the γ phase is represented as viewed from the copper edge, or equivalently, from the β space, because the opposite side is not well understood (Fig. 136). The several curves on its surface correspond

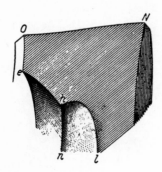

Fig. 136.

State space of γ solid solution as seen from the copper corner.

to those appearing in Figs. 131, 133, and 134 so that a complete description is unnecessary.

Between these various homogeneous spaces there exist two- and three-phase regions. Their forms are determined by the forms of the homogeneous spaces which they connect. Detailed analysis of these spaces will not be made. However, the $\alpha + \beta + \gamma$ region is worthy of comment. It has been noted that the three curves, gi, fk, and hl, which bound this region, all pass through a maximum. These three maxima lie in a line on one conode, a situation which means that the whole state space at this point has shrunk to a straight line. It lies, in Fig. 134, between the lines $g'h'$ and $g''h''$. On either side of this conode, the conode triangles have an arrangement as if one were reflected from the other in a mirror.

4. Sections Through the Space Diagram

In order to obtain a more complete view of the equilibria which occur in the ternary system, we shall consider, as usual, a series of isothermal sections at different temperatures. After the primary solidification of the α phase is in progress, but before that of the β and γ phases have set in, the section has a very simple form. At the copper corner there is a region of homogeneous α substance and adjoining it a band-shaped two-phase region of α+melt. Beyond this band the field of homogeneous melt extends over the remaining portion of the triangle. After freezing has progressed to a lower temperature, there appears, in addition to the α region, one of homogeneous β extending out from a side of the concentration triangle. Besides the fields $s+\alpha$, $s+\beta$, and $\alpha+\beta$, there originates during solidification the three-phase field $s+\alpha+\beta$ in an arrangement analogous to that of Fig. 67 (p. 78), except that the letters α and β should be interchanged. With decreasing temperature, the β field extends itself until it reaches in a broad band across the triangle in a manner somewhat like the α band of Fig. 68 (p. 78). This band is separated from the α field by a two-phase band of $\alpha+\beta$. At this temperature the α substance is no longer in equilibrium with the melt. When the pre-

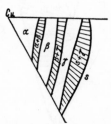

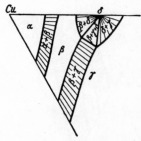

FIG. 137. Isothermal section after the solidification of the α, β, and γ phases.

FIG. 138. Isothermal section in the temperature range of the transformations in the solid state.

cipitation of γ crystals begins, configurations appear between the β and γ fields which are similar to those previously existing between the α and β fields. After the field of the γ phase has extended itself across the triangle, but before the temperature has dropped to the point where transformations occur in the solid state, the isothermal section appears as shown in Fig. 137. The position of the boundaries between solid and melt ceases to be of interest at this point since the low-copper phases are not to be considered here.

In the course of further cooling, the temperature will cross the line $c_1 d_1 e_1$ (Fig. 134). Since the temperature will still be above ag and gi, the boundary curve of the field of α solid solution will still be of the continuous type (Fig. 131), because the α phase is for all compositions in equilibrium with the β phase. The boundary curve between the homogeneous β phase and that of the two-phase region $\alpha+\beta$ must likewise be continuous for the same reason, as shown in Fig. 138. On the

side farther from the copper corner, the region of β phase has already
encountered the line fc (Fig. 134), with the result that its boundary curve
has a discontinuity. This situation arises because the β material stands
in equilibrium with the γ phase for some compositions, whereas for others
it is in equilibrium with the δ substance. The three two-phase regions
$\beta+\gamma$, $\beta+\delta$, $\delta+\gamma$ are separated by the three-phase region $\beta+\gamma+\delta$ in
agreement with the general law stated in the supplement to Chapter II
that two-phase regions cannot adjoin each other.

For further lowering of the temperature below the maximum point,
x, on the curve gxi (Fig. 131) but still above the invariant equilibrium, g,
the α phase is in equilibrium with the γ phase over a small interval in
the vicinity of x; over the larger part of this boundary curve, however,

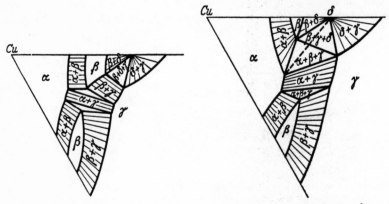

Figs. 139 and 140. Isothermal sections in the temperature range of the transformations in the solid state.

it is still in equilibrium with the β material. Correspondingly, Fig. 139
shows a gap in the β field within which there is equilibrium between α
and γ. In this gap there are also two three-phase regions $(\alpha+\beta+\gamma)_1$
and $(\alpha+\beta+\gamma)_2$, in which the same phases participate but with different
compositions in each triangle. The remaining part of the section is
similar to Fig. 138.

As the temperature drops still further, the interval between the two
triangles widens, as may be seen from Fig. 133, while simultaneously the
interval between the points of intersection of the isothermal plane with
the curves kf and cf (Fig. 134) diminishes. The paths of these intersection
points (actually kf and cf) meet at the point f after a sufficient lowering
of the temperature. Thus the two triangles $\alpha+\beta+\gamma$ and $\beta+\gamma+\delta$, as
shown in Fig. 140, come into contact to form the four-phase quadrilateral
pictured in Fig. 134.

As mentioned previously above, the combinations in which both β and γ participate cannot exist below the invariant plane. Hence, as the temperature continues to fall, the quadrilateral illustrated in Fig. 140 splits along the dotted line into the two triangles, $\beta+\alpha+\delta$ and $\alpha+\gamma+\delta$. For a small additional drop in temperature (not, however, below a of Fig. 131 or b of Fig. 133), the isothermal section takes on the appearance illustrated in Fig. 141, where for the first time the α solid solution is found in equilibrium with the δ substance. This figure shows that the α phase participates in two-phase equilibria with all three other phases and that there are two $\alpha+\beta$ phase fields.

When the temperature drops below that of points a (Fig. 131) and b (Fig. 133) the region of β crystals on the tin side disappears and with it those phase fields in which the β substance existed. The space of the mixture of α and δ crystals then extends to the copper-tin side of the concentration triangle, with the result that the form of the section is much simplified (Fig. 142).

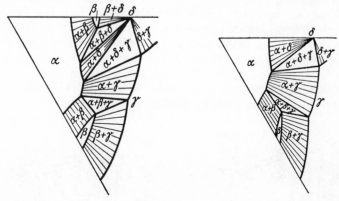

FIGS. 141 and 142. Isothermal sections in the temperature range of the transformations in the solid state.

The section has now assumed the form which persists down to ordinary temperature, with the qualification that the triangle $\alpha+\beta+\gamma$ will slowly approach more closely to the zinc-copper side. There remain only the two three-phase triangles, $\alpha+\gamma+\delta$ and $\alpha+\beta+\gamma$. They are separated from each other by the two-phase area $\alpha+\gamma$.

As the reader will have noted, this discussion has assumed that the γ crystals persist, in the high-tin alloys, down to ordinary temperature. The facts are otherwise, for there is a series of complicated transformations in the ternary system (see Fig. 128) which cannot be readily explained. At the present time, only two regions of the ternary system are reasonably clear—namely, the tin-rich part, in which the α and δ

phases are in equilibrium with each other, and the high-zinc region in
which the γ phase is stable at ordinary temperature. In the last-
mentioned portion, the α phase can exist in equilibrium with the γ substance, but how far this situation extends toward the tin side is not
known. The first case is illustrated by the red brasses and the second,
by the tin-containing special brasses which are of considerable industrial
value.

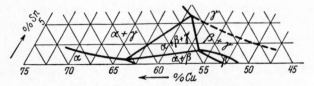

FIG. 143. Crystalline types in the tin-poor tin-zinc-copper alloys
at low temperatures.

Fig. 143 shows the actual boundaries of several fields in the high-zinc
part of the ternary system at about 400° C. Because of the importance
of this region, three vertical sections are shown in Figs. 144, 145, and
146, corresponding respectively to 1.25, 2.5, and 7 per cent of tin.[9] The
first vertical section is so located that it intersects the region of homogeneous β phase at low temperature, whereas the second and third sections
do not.

The first section (Fig. 144) resembles the zinc-copper diagram in its
principal features, except that three-phase fields appear in place of

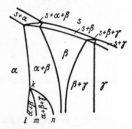

FIG. 144. Partial section in the tin-zinc-
copper system for a constant tin
content of 1.25 per cent.

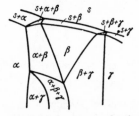

FIG. 145. Partial section in the tin-zinc-
copper system for a constant tin
content of 2.5 per cent.

peritectic straight lines. Furthermore, between the α and $\alpha+\beta$ fields
there are two other regions in which occur, respectively, mixtures of
α and γ and of α, β, and γ phases. These regions come into existence at
relatively low temperature by the intersection of the vertical plane with
the curve ix (Fig. 131). Since this curve specifies the compositions of
α solid solution which are in equilibrium simultaneously with β and γ, it

follows that the three-phase field must touch the α region in this inter-section. In other words, adjoining the α space are the two regions *lkm* and *mkn* (Fig. 144) in which exist, respectively, the mixtures $\alpha+\gamma$ and $\alpha+\beta+\gamma$. At higher temperatures these two fields move closer to the copper-tin side, as may be seen from the form of the α and β spaces (Figs. 133 and 134) and hence leave the plane of the vertical section. The structure of the alloys of this section is therefore very similar to that of ordinary brass except for the small interval ln where the γ phase appears.

The section shown in Fig. 145 no longer encounters the β field at low temperature. This substance appears here only as a constituent of the

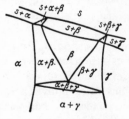

Fig. 146.

Partial section in the tin-zinc-copper system for a constant tin content of 7 per cent.

three-phase field, $\alpha+\beta+\gamma$. It is no longer an independently formed structural constituent at low temperature. This condition agrees with the observed fact that in brasses containing more than 2 per cent tin, no primary β crystals are to be found.

The section of Fig. 146 is no longer in contact with the three-phase triangle $\alpha+\beta+\gamma$ at low temperature and, correspondingly, the β phase is not to be found. The alloys of this field are considered to be beyond the region of special brasses.

Chapter XI

The Allotropic Forms of Iron in the Ternary System

A. Introduction. Statement of the Problem

In the solid state iron possesses three modifications generally termed α, γ, and δ. The α form exists from room temperature to about 906° C; between 906 and 1401° C the γ variety prevails; above the latter temperature and persisting to the melting point is the δ modification.

The γ form has a face-centered lattice, whereas the α and δ modifications are body-centered. In fact, all the evidence indicates that the latter two forms are structurally identical. The situation may be regarded as the interruption of one phase field by the entrance of another—γ iron in this case. This concept fits in with the fact that in the ternary alloys with which we shall shortly be concerned, instances occur in which the γ region disappears and the α and δ regions merge.

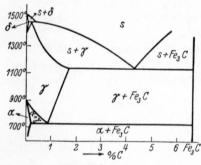

Fig. 147. Diagram of the iron-carbon alloys.

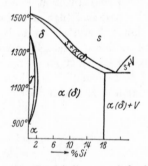

Fig. 148. Partial diagram of the iron-silicon alloys.

In binary alloys, the transformations in iron may be influenced in either of two ways; the introduction of the second element may widen the γ field or may cause it to become narrower and disappear. The most familiar example of the first case is presented by the iron-carbon system of which the constitutional diagram is shown in Fig. 147. (The stable graphite system is omitted from consideration.) Obviously, the range of γ solid solution in starting out from pure iron is extended both upward and downward. The δ field is isolated in the solidification range

154

so that a later combination with the α field is impossible. In contrast with this type of system there are others—for example, the iron-silicon alloys, which exhibit a very different behavior in this respect. Fig. 148 shows that the γ region is constricted with increasing silicon content and vanishes entirely at about 2 per cent silicon.

Examination of the diagram of Fig. 148 shows that it differs in two respects from Fig. 147. First, in no instance is the γ phase formed directly from the melt, as is the case for certain compositions of the iron-carbon alloys. Secondly, the γ region vanishes before it comes into contact with another crystalline phase—such as iron silicide. Disregarding the fact that the boundary curve of the γ region terminates at both ends in the pure component iron, the γ "bulge," as it is frequently called, presents nothing unusual. The γ crystals show at a definite temperature a maximum solubility for silicon, a situation which occurs in many other cases of limited miscibility.

It is obvious that if two binary systems involving iron and one other component and having configurations like those shown in Figs. 147 and

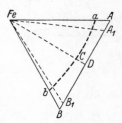

FIG. 149.

Triangle of concentrations of the partial system Fe*AB*.

148 are combined in a ternary system, then the one arrangement must somehow pass over into the other. On the other hand, these configurations are so dissimilar that at first glance a transformation from one into the other appears impossible. The problem, which we are about to undertake, of making this transition is one of special interest in the theory of ternary systems. In recent years it has been studied by E. Scheil[10] and also in the numerous investigations of the ternary systems of iron by R. Vogel[11] and W. Köster[12] and their co-workers.

In a ternary system, both the nature of the diagram and the structure of the alloys must evidently depend upon the character of the substances added. The type of binary diagram which the added components make with each other differs from one case to another, and may in the ternary system cause serious complications which have no essential connection with the problem we are attempting to solve. Under the circumstances, the simplest case will be assumed—that is, the two constituents added to iron form with each other an unbroken series of solid solutions. This solid solution phase, which is assumed to extend for some distance into the ternary system, will be designated by C.

The apparent difficulty in attempting to get from a diagram like the one shown in Fig. 147 to another like that of Fig. 148 lies principally in the fact that both these figures illustrate binary systems. In ternary systems there is an added variable, and there are correspondingly more possibilities of transition, as has been observed previously. The concentration triangle of the hypothetical system is shown in Fig. 149. Concerning this triangle only one definite statement can be made—namely, that the boundary of the C solid solution must run in some fashion along a curve ab which may possess discontinuities. The transition of the system shown in Fig. 147 into that illustrated in Fig. 148 will be traced by the use of a number of vertical sections all passing through

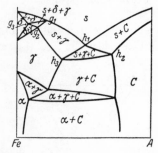

FIG. 150. Section FeA_1 (Fig. 149).

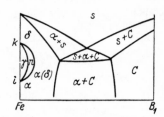

FIG. 151. Section FeB_1 (Fig. 149).

the iron corner of the triangle. In the vicinity of the side FeA, which corresponds to the diagram in Fig. 147, the vertical sections still have approximately the same form but have been modified into the ternary type. Such a section is illustrated in Fig. 150. It differs from the one shown in Fig. 147, principally in having the invariant isothermal three-phase lines replaced by regions of three-phase equilibrium corresponding to

$$s + \delta \rightleftarrows \gamma,$$
$$s \rightleftarrows \gamma + C,$$
$$\gamma \rightleftarrows \alpha + C.$$

Fig. 151 shows the nature of the transformation which occurs in the diagram of Fig. 148 as the vertical section moves into the position FeB_1. Again the most important change is that the invariant equilibrium of the isothermal line has been replaced by an area of three-phase equilibrium, $s + \alpha + C$.

Comparison of the diagrams in Figs. 150 and 151 reveals that they differ from each other with respect to the form and boundary of the γ

field in two ways, just as do the corresponding binary systems. In Fig. 151, the γ area is completely surrounded by the α (δ) region, whereas in Fig. 150 it is in contact with both the C crystals and the melt. The explanation will be facilitated by dividing the transformation into two steps through the introduction between Figs. 150 and 151 of the intermediate vertical section shown in Fig. 152. In this figure the solid solution γ occurs in contact with C but not with the melt.

The next section will consider the transition from Fig. 151 to Fig. 152 and a later one, the further change to Fig. 150.

B. Restriction of the γ Space in the Solid State

1. State Spaces

The α and δ crystals are taken to be fundamentally identical. Hence a change from the α to the δ field must take place in a continuous manner. As the section under consideration (Fig. 152) approaches the side FeB of the triangle (Fig. 149) the points a and b and likewise the points c and d must move toward each other and finally merge. Since α and

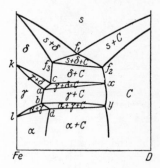

Fig. 152.

Type of section intermediate between Figs. 150 and 151.

δ are identical, the space curves which these terminal points describe must not form kinks when they meet, but must produce continuous curves.

The part of the state space of homogeneous γ substance which lies between the sections shown in Figs. 151 and 152 has the form shown in Fig. 153 where the observer is looking from within the ternary space toward the Fe corner. On the surface of this space are two ribs am and bm, which as they approach the side FeB merge and disappear. The curve knl lies on the side FeB and kaobl is in the plane of the cut FeD. The rib amb fades back into the surface and disappears at m, which is so located that the tangent to the curve is vertical at this point. It is evident that the γ solid solution is saturated with different substances over the two surfaces aknlbm and aobm. The first surface indicates the temperature and composition of γ phase saturated with α(δ) substance and the second gives the same information about γ substance saturated with *C*. In other words, the surface *aknlbm* is the boundary between the region of the homogeneous γ phase and the two-phase region of γ+α (δ), and *aobm* is similarly related to the two-phase space of γ+*C*. These two state spaces cannot adjoin each other but, as the supplement to Chapter II pointed out, must be separated by a three-phase space. In this case the three-phase space is α (δ) +*C*+γ, which touches the γ region along the curve *amb* and is intersected twice by the vertical section Fe*D*, with the consequent production of the two curve-sided triangles, *acx* and *bdy* (Fig. 152).

The depicted form of the state space of *C* (Fig. 154) must be similar to that of the γ solid solution. Certain compositions of the *C* phase are in equilibrium with α and others with the γ phase. Corresponding to the rib *aobm* of Fig. 153, there is a rib *a'o'b'm'* on the boundary surface of the *C* substance space (Fig. 154). To each point on the surface *aobm* there is a corresponding point on the surface *a'o'b'm'* which is connected

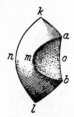

Fig. 153. Space of γ solid solution between the sections shown in Figs. 151 and 152.

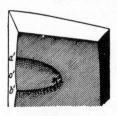

Fig. 154. Space of C substance between the sections of Figs. 151 and 152.

to the first by a conode. This fact naturally holds for the points on both bounding curves. The part of the two-phase space of γ and *C* crystals which is under consideration is bounded on one side by the cut Fe*D*—that is, by a vertical plane—and on the other by a surface which is generated by the motion of a conode having its ends on the curves *amb* and *a'm'b'*. Its ends are closed by the surfaces *aobm* and *a'o'b'm'*. Hence this space has the form of a horizontal cylinder which has been sectioned lengthwise by the Fe*D* plane.

In Chapter II it was shown that a surface generated by the motion of a conode corresponds to a boundary surface between a two-phase and a three-phase space. The present case involves the boundary of the three-phase space α (δ) +γ+*C*, which is developed by the motion of a conode having its ends on the curves *amb* and *a'm'b'*. The boundary of such a space has the form of a three-edged tube and is developed by the motion of a horizontal conode triangle. A space of this kind generally terminates either in the isothermal plane of a four-phase equilibrium or on a side of the prism of state where it shrinks to a straight line. In the present example we are not considering a complete phase space—and this remark holds for the other spaces—but only that part to one side of the arbitrarily located plane Fe*D*. The intersection of this plane with the three-phase space, $\alpha+\gamma+C$, forms the three-cornered areas, *acx* and *bdy*, shown in Fig. 152. These areas inclose, on this section, the

Fig. 155.

Space of the mixture of γ and C between the sections shown in Figs. 151 and 152 when looked at from the side Fe*A* (Fig. 149).

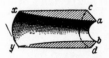

two-phase area $\gamma+C$. Actually, on the Fe*B* side of the plane Fe*D*, the three-cornered $\alpha\,(\delta)+\gamma+C$ space surrounds the $\gamma+C$ region. When looked at from the side Fe*A*, this partial three-phase space has the form depicted in Fig. 155. Since the cut Fe*D* has been located by chance, the lines *xc*, *xa*, *yb*, and *yd* are not conodes; neither are they in general, straight lines or isotherms.

A two-phase space of $\gamma+\alpha(\delta)$ adjoins the part of the state space of γ crystals which is outside the surface *aobm* (Fig. 153). This two-phase space is bounded on the side opposite the γ region partly by the α phase region and partly, on the surface *cabd*, by the $\alpha+\gamma+C$ region. It has

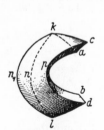

Fig. 156. Two-phase space $\alpha(\delta)+\gamma$ as seen when looked at toward the iron corner.

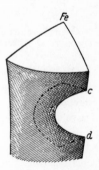

Fig. 157. Space of $\alpha\,(\delta)$ solid solution between the sections of Figs. 151 and 152.

the shape shown in Fig. 156. As usual in these figures, the lettering of the various points agrees with the characters in Figs. 153-157. The space form shown in Fig. 156 surrounds the region pictured in Fig. 153. It can be imagined to originate from the movement of the triangle *kca* in such a manner that the corner, *c*, glides along the curve *cd* and the corner *a*, along *ab*; meanwhile two curves, *knl* and *kn₁l*, are generated by *k*, with the result that a four-sided figure is developed. One sees that the boundary surface *acpdb* adjoining the three-phase space $\alpha+\gamma+C$ does not extend to the side FeB, as indeed it could not because this three-phase space does not appear there.

The homogeneous α space surrounds the two-phase α (δ) $+\gamma$ region. In the section FeD it is separated from the $\delta+C$ field by the curve cf_3. Along the curve cpd (Fig. 156) it touches the $\alpha+\gamma+C$ region. For the one-phase α territory to have contact with this three-phase space over a surface is not possible, as was seen in Chapter II; Fig. 152 shows that the two are separated by the two-phase $\alpha+C$ region. Toward the FeB_1 side, the α substance separates the $\alpha+C$ space from the $\alpha+\gamma$ territory, except that the two two-phase regions touch along the curve cpd. From this analysis it will be deduced that the α region has approximately the form shown in Fig. 157, as seen when the observer looks toward the Fe corner. From this figure the reader may imagine how the cavity containing the

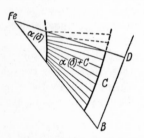

Fig. 158. Isothermal section above the temperature of γ phase.

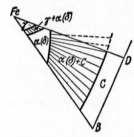

Fig. 159. Isothermal section between k and c in Fig. 152.

space $\alpha+\gamma$, and within that, the γ space, closes progressively toward the side FeB. Above, the space is limited by the solidus surface. Below, it extends to room temperature, although in Fig. 157 the lower part has been cut off to save space. The dotted curve indicates how the cavity in which the γ and $\gamma+\alpha$ regions lie, extends into the interior of the α space, corresponding to Fig. 156.

The transition from the configuration in Fig. 151 into that of Fig. 152 has now been followed out completely. The state spaces which have been established may be listed as follows:

(1) Three homogeneous regions comprising the γ, C, and α (δ) phases (Figs. 153, 154, and 157).

(2) Three two-phase spaces $\gamma+C$, $\gamma+\alpha(\delta)$ (Fig. 156), and $\alpha(\delta)+C$.

(3) A three-phase space $\alpha(\delta)+\gamma+C$ (Fig. 155).

2. Isothermal Sections

In order to obtain the clearest possible picture of the various configurations, let us consider several isothermal sections. The freezing process is

of no interest in the part of the concentration triangle marked out by
Fe*DB*; hence, the discussion may be limited to the solid state. The first
section will be taken above the γ region (Fig. 158) and in it, as in the
following diagrams, the part of the boundary curves outside the selected
line Fe*D* will be dotted to show that this plane has no fundamental
significance.

The picture is very simple.* Besides the two homogeneous regions of
α and *C* crystals, only the two-phase region α(δ) + *C* is cut by this plane.
Obviously, the direction of the conodes need not agree with that of the
line Fe*D*. A similar diagram is obtained by a section taken below the
γ field. We may next consider a section taken below *k* but above *c* (Fig.
152). The shape of the boundary curves can be obtained from an examination of the various state spaces. Since the γ space (Fig. 153) has
been cut above *a*, the boundary line of this field will be a continuous curve.

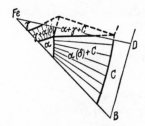

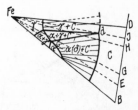

Fig. 160. Isothermal section between *c*
and *a* in Fig. 152.

Fig. 161. Isothermal section between *a*
and *b* in Fig. 152.

Since the cut is also above *c* (Fig. 156), this condition holds also for the
outer boundary of the region of α+γ. Furthermore, no kink can be observed in the boundary between the two-phase field of α+*C* and the α
region. Contact between the γ space and the two-phase region of γ+*C*
does not occur, for at this temperature the γ field is completely surrounded
by α substance. Hence, the isothermal section shown in Fig. 159 does not
differ much from the one in Fig. 158 except that inside of the α field there
are the γ and γ+α regions.

A section taken below *c* but above *a* (Fig. 152) will have the outlines
illustrated in Fig. 160. On the basis of Fig. 153, it may be assumed that
the γ field is bounded by a continuous curve. Such an assumption for the
field α+γ would be an error, however, since in this section the ribs *ca* and
cp (Fig. 156) are encountered, and the boundary curve must possess a
discontinuity. On opposite sides of the discontinuity, the γ+α field must
be in equilibrium with different phase aggregates. On the left of the kink
it is adjacent to the α space because the surface of separation in this case

---

* Note by translator: Fig. 158 appears to be in error if the actual instead of the
schematic situation is considered. To avoid the γ space, the isothermal plane must
lie at 1400° C or above, yet at this temperature the plane would surely encounter
the space of liquid metal.

is $n_1 kcp$ (Fig. 156). On the right it is separated from the $\alpha + \gamma + C$ mixture by the surface $acpdb$.

For a temperature between the points a and b (Fig. 152), the isothermal section appears as in Fig. 161. The boundary curve of the γ region now has a kink, for it borders on two different two-phase fields—namely, $\gamma + C$ and $\alpha + \gamma$. The complete conode triangle is revealed by the section of the three-phase space (Fig. 155) by the isothermal plane. Its corners touch the homogeneous phase spaces α, γ, and C.

Starting out from the point a (Fig. 152), the conode triangle $\gamma + \alpha + C$ moves toward the side FeB as the temperature falls (Fig. 161), but does not reach it and later returns toward the plane FeD. When the temperature has fallen below b (Fig. 152), the isothermal section again resembles Fig. 160 and still later assumes a configuration similar to Fig. 159.

The isothermal sections are not difficult to understand. Study of them is complicated only because one side, FeD, of the triangle being analyzed is located arbitrarily and represents no theoretically important boundary.

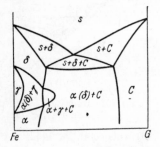

Fig. 162.

Section FeG (Fig. 161).

Account has been taken of this fact by extending some of the boundaries as dotted lines beyond the FeD plane. The exposition which has been made in the foregoing paragraphs serves as an example of how selected portions of a diagram can be analyzed and how the apparent difficulties which arise from considering only a fraction of the system may be overcome.

In the following discussion of vertical sections it will be observed how complicated they are and how little they contribute to a thorough understanding of the case. This condition results because the vertical sections have no physical or phase theoretical significance, whereas the isothermal sections give an insight into the equilibria existing in the system. The only advantage which they offer is the possibility of following, experimentally, the state of a given alloy at different temperatures.

3. Vertical Sections

We shall limit the discussion to sections passing through the Fe corner of the concentration triangle, as shown in Fig. 161. This figure will be assumed to correspond to the temperature at which the conode triangle approaches most closely the side Fe*B*, or, in other words, to the temperature at which the curve *cpd* (Fig. 156) becomes tangent to a vertical plane passing through the Fe corner (that is, through the *kl* corner). We shall also assume that the curve *ab* becomes tangent at the same temperature to another vertical plane through the Fe corner. This assumption is not at all necessary but does simplify the discussion.

The vertical sections of the part Fe*EB* (Fig. 161) show nothing important in addition to what was indicated in Fig. 151. Phase combinations in which γ and C appear together do not occur.

The section Fe*G* has the form illustrated by Fig. 162. The γ field still has a continuous curve as its boundary and is completely surrounded by the $\alpha+\gamma$ region. The three-phase space (Fig. 155) has already made its appearance, but as a comparison of Figs. 155 and 161 will demonstrate,

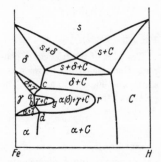

FIG. 163. Section Fe*H* (Fig. 161).

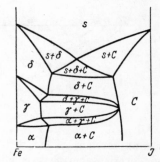

FIG. 164. Section Fe*J* (Fig. 161).

the rib *cd* has been intersected twice, whereas ribs *ab* and *xy* lie completely outside of this cut. Hence, in this section the space of $\alpha+\gamma+C$ is bounded by two curves, one of which is the trace of the outer surface of this space on the vertical plane and the other is produced by the intersection of the plane with the surface *abdc* (Fig. 155).

The section Fe*H* (Fig. 163) differs from the previous one in that it intersects the region $\gamma+C$. Since the side *a'm'b'* of the C phase space (Fig. 154) has not been reached, whereas the curve *amb* (Fig. 153) is intersected at two points, the cross-section of the state space of $\gamma+C$ made by the plane Fe*H* has the form *agb* (Fig. 163). The outer boundary surface of the region $\alpha+\gamma+C$ is cut in such a way as to produce a curve similar to *agb*. In this section the two regions $\gamma+C$ and $\alpha+\gamma+C$ have not yet touched the region of homogeneous C crystals.

The more nearly the position of the cut approaches the line Fe*J*, the farther the two regions $\gamma+C$ and $\alpha+\gamma+C$ extend to the right, and this is particularly true for the area *agb* (Fig. 163). As is immediately obvious in Fig. 161, the distance between g and r decreases as the extension takes place. In the section FeJ (Fig. 164) the points g and r have simultaneously attained the boundary curve of the C region. For planes nearer to FeD, the two three-phase areas move apart until the section of Fig. 152 is attained.

C. Separation of the Space of the γ Crystals From the Solidus Surface

We shall now proceed to an analysis of the transition from the diagram of Fig. 150 to that of Fig. 152. The principal difference between these two diagrams is that in Fig. 150 there are two three-phase equilibria involving the melt—namely, $s+\delta+\gamma$ and $s+\gamma+C$—whereas in Fig. 152 there exists only one such three-phase region—specifically, $s+\delta+C$.

The transition can proceed through an invariant four-phase equilibrium in which the phases s, α, γ, and C participate. In Chapter VI an explana-

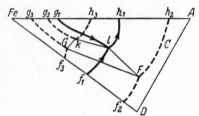

Fig. 165.

The part of the triangle of concentrations which lies between the sections of Figs. 150 and 151. The process of freezing.

tion was given of the fact that four three-phase equilibrium spaces adjoin any invariant four-phase equilibrium. In the system under discussion the four three-phase regions are: $s+\delta+\gamma$, $s+\gamma+C$, $s+\delta+C$, and $\delta+\gamma+C$. In the eutectic case the invariant reaction is: $s \rightleftarrows \delta+\gamma+C$, whereas in a peritectic arrangement one of three reactions may occur:

$$s+\delta \rightleftarrows \gamma+C,$$
$$s+\gamma \rightleftarrows \delta+C,$$
$$s+C \rightleftarrows \gamma+\delta.$$

Since, according to the diagram, δ but not γ exists at high temperatures, whereas at lower temperatures the γ phase but not the δ occurs, the first peritectic reaction must be the one which prevails.

We shall assume that the transformation is a peritectic one and that the four-phase equilibrium is approached from above by the three-phase spaces $s+\delta+\gamma$ and $s+\delta+C$ and from below by $s+\gamma+C$ and $\delta+\gamma+C$. In other words, the temperature of the invariant equilibrium lies below the three-phase fields $s+\delta+\gamma$ (Fig. 150) and $s+\delta+C$ (Fig. 152) and above the field $s+\gamma+C$ (Fig. 150). The curves of doubly saturated liquid will therefore have the positions given in Fig. 165, which brings to mind the configuration discussed in part C of Chapter IV. Such an arrangement is possible here since the system possesses a limited degree of solid solubility. Corresponding points of Figs. 150, 152, and 165 are all marked with the same letters. The compositions of the crystalline phases participating in the equilibria are outlined by the dotted curves. From the form of the quadrilateral $GklF$ of invariant equilibrium, one notes that the system undergoes a peritectic reaction in which the two phases, melt l and δ phase G, give place to the γ phase of composition k and C phase of composition F. The liquidus surface is represented schematically in Fig. 166.

For the discussion of Fig. 165, it is advantageous to employ the binary side FeA (Fig. 147) rather than the section diagram lying within the ternary system (Fig. 150). The principal difference between the diagrams is that instead of the ternary fields $g_1g_2g_3$ *and* $h_1h_2h_3$ of Fig. 150, hori-

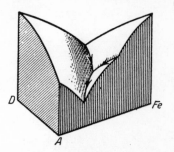

FIG. 166.

   Space diagram corresponding to Fig. 165.

zontal straight lines, one peritectic and one eutectic, are in evidence. This change has no influence on the discussion. In the part Feg_3GFf_2, the γ phase is not in contact with the liquid alloy; the δ substance is in equilibrium with the melt in this field.

The transition from the configuration of Fig. 150 to that of Fig. 152 has now been accomplished. The circumstance of there being a γ field at lower temperatures in the latter diagram has nothing to do with the present problem and offers no difficulty. This field exists because the boundaries of the spaces of the different crystalline phases descend, as the temperature decreases, in such a way that the α field which extends up to the Fe corner as shown in Fig. 150, widens out from there to the side FeD (Fig. 165).

Since the transformations of the remaining structural features of Figs. 150, 151, and 152 are essentially straightforward, no further details will be discussed.

Bibliography

1. Guertler, W., "Betrachtungen zur theoretischen Metallhüttenkunde," *Met. u. Erz.*, **8**, 192-195 (1920).

2. Fuss, V., "Die Konstitution der aluminiumreichen Al-Fe-Si-Legierungen," *Ztschr. Metallk.*, **23**, 231-236 (1931).

3. This footnote calls attention to references 4 and 5.

4. Gwyer, A. G. C., and Phillips, H. W. L., "The Constitution of Alloys of Aluminum with Silicon and Iron," *J. Inst. Met.*, **38**, 29-81 (1927).

5. Dix, E. H., Jr., "A Note on the Microstructure of Aluminum-Iron Alloys of High Purity," *Proc. Am. Soc. Test. Mat.*, **25**, part 2, 120-129 (1925).

6. Tammann, G., and Hansen, M., "Über das ternäre System Kupfer-Zinn-Zink," *Ztschr. anorg. Chem.*, **138**, 137-161 (1934).

7. Bauer, O., and Vollenbruck, O., "Das Erstarrungs- und Umwandlungschaubild der Kupfer-Zinnlegierungen," *Mitt. Materialprüfungsamt*, **40**, 181-215 (1922).

8. Hamasumi, M., and Nishigori, S., "The Equilibrium Diagram of Copper-Tin Alloys," *World Eng. Congr. Tokyo*, paper 698 (1929); *Proceedings*, **36**, 211 (1931).

9. Bauer, O., and Hansen, M., "Der Einfluss von dritten Metallen auf die Konstitution der Messinglegierungen. III—Der Einfluss von Zinn," *Ztschr. Metallk.*, **22**, 387-391, 405-411 (1931); **23**, 19-22 (1931).

10. Scheil, Erich, "Über ternäre Diagramme auf der Grundlage Eisen-Kohlenstoff," *Mitt. Forsch.-Inst. Ver. Stahlw. A.-G.* (Dortmund), **1**, 1-21 (1928).

11. Occasional references to R. Vogel's work appear in *Stahl u. Eisen* beginning with vol. **37**, 1917.

12. Articles or abstracts on various iron alloys under the authorship of W. Köster appear in *Stahl u. Eisen*, **51** (1931) and **52** (1932).

Index

CATALOG OF DOVER BOOKS

BOOKS EXPLAINING SCIENCE AND MATHEMATICS

THE COMMON SENSE OF THE EXACT SCIENCES, W. K. Clifford. Introduction by James Newman, edited by Karl Pearson. For 70 years this has been a guide to classical scientific and mathematical thought. Explains with unusual clarity basic concepts, such as extension of meaning of symbols, characteristics of surface boundaries, properties of plane figures, vectors, Cartesian method of determining position, etc. Long preface by Bertrand Russell. Bibliography of Clifford. Corrected, 130 diagrams redrawn. 249pp. 5⅜ x 8.
T61 Paperbound **$1.60**

SCIENCE THEORY AND MAN, Erwin Schrödinger. This is a complete and unabridged reissue of SCIENCE AND THE HUMAN TEMPERAMENT plus an additional essay: "What is an Elementary Particle?" Nobel Laureate Schrödinger discusses such topics as nature of scientific method, the nature of science, chance and determinism, science and society, conceptual models for physical entities, elementary particles and wave mechanics. Presentation is popular and may be followed by most people with little or no scientific training. "Fine practical preparation for a time when laws of nature, human institutions . . . are undergoing a critical examination without parallel," Waldemar Kaempffert, N. Y. TIMES. 192pp. 5⅜ x 8.
T428 Paperbound **$1.35**

PIONEERS OF SCIENCE, O. Lodge. Eminent scientist-expositor's authoritative, yet elementary survey of great scientific theories. Concentrating on individuals—Copernicus, Brahe, Kepler, Galileo, Descartes, Newton, Laplace, Herschel, Lord Kelvin, and other scientists—the author presents their discoveries in historical order adding biographical material on each man and full, specific explanations of their achievements. The clear and complete treatment of the post-Newtonian astronomers is a feature seldom found in other books on the subject. Index. 120 illustrations. xv + 404pp. 5⅜ x 8.
T716 Paperbound **$1.50**

THE EVOLUTION OF SCIENTIFIC THOUGHT FROM NEWTON TO EINSTEIN, A. d'Abro. Einstein's special and general theories of relativity, with their historical implications, are analyzed in non-technical terms. Excellent accounts of the contributions of Newton, Riemann, Weyl, Planck, Eddington, Maxwell, Lorentz and others are treated in terms of space and time, equations of electromagnetics, finiteness of the universe, methodology of science. 21 diagrams. 482pp. 5⅜ x 8.
T2 Paperbound **$2.00**

THE RISE OF THE NEW PHYSICS, A. d'Abro. A half-million word exposition, formerly titled THE DECLINE OF MECHANISM, for readers not versed in higher mathematics. The only thorough explanation, in everyday language, of the central core of modern mathematical physical theory, treating both classical and modern theoretical physics, and presenting in terms almost anyone can understand the equivalent of 5 years of study of mathematical physics. Scientifically impeccable coverage of mathematical-physical thought from the Newtonian system up through the electronic theories of Dirac and Heisenberg and Fermi's statistics. Combines both history and exposition; provides a broad yet unified and detailed view, with constant comparison of classical and modern views on phenomena and theories. "A must for anyone doing serious study in the physical sciences," JOURNAL OF THE FRANKLIN INSTITUTE. "Extraordinary faculty . . . to explain ideas and theories of theoretical physics in the language of daily life," ISIS. First part of set covers philosophy of science, drawing upon the practice of Newton, Maxwell, Poincaré, Einstein, others, discussing modes of thought, experiment, interpretations of causality, etc. In the second part, 100 pages explain grammar and vocabulary of mathematics, with discussions of functions, groups, series, Fourier series, etc. The remainder is devoted to concrete, detailed coverage of both classical and quantum physics, explaining such topics as analytic mechanics, Hamilton's principle, wave theory of light, electromagnetic waves, groups of transformations, thermodynamics, phase rule, Brownian movement, kinetics, special relativity, Planck's original quantum theory, Bohr's atom, Zeeman effect, Broglie's wave mechanics, Heisenberg's uncertainty, Eigen-values, matrices, scores of other important topics. Discoveries and theories are covered for such men as Alembert, Born, Cantor, Debye, Euler, Foucault, Galois, Gauss, Hadamard, Kelvin, Kepler, Laplace, Maxwell, Pauli, Rayleigh, Volterra, Weyl, Young, more than 180 others. Indexed. 97 illustrations. ix + 982pp. 5⅜ x 8.
T3 Volume 1, Paperbound **$2.00**
T4 Volume 2, Paperbound **$2.00**

CONCERNING THE NATURE OF THINGS, Sir William Bragg. Christmas lectures delivered at the Royal Society by Nobel laureate. Why a spinning ball travels in a curved track; how uranium is transmuted to lead, etc. Partial contents: atoms, gases, liquids, crystals, metals, etc. No scientific background needed; wonderful for intelligent child. 32pp. of photos, 57 figures. xii + 232pp. 5⅜ x 8.
T31 Paperbound **$1.35**

THE UNIVERSE OF LIGHT, Sir William Bragg. No scientific training needed to read Nobel Prize winner's expansion of his Royal Institute Christmas Lectures. Insight into nature of light, methods and philosophy of science. Explains lenses, reflection, color, resonance, polarization, x-rays, the spectrum, Newton's work with prisms, Huygens' with polarization, Crookes' with cathode ray, etc. Leads into clear statement of 2 major historical theories of light, corpuscle and wave. Dozens of experiments you can do. 199 illus., including 2 full-page color plates. 293pp. 5⅜ x 8.
S538 Paperbound **$1.85**

PHYSICS, THE PIONEER SCIENCE, L. W. Taylor. First thorough text to place all important physical phenomena in cultural-historical framework; remains best work of its kind. Exposition of physical laws, theories developed chronologically, with great historical, illustrative experiments diagrammed, described, worked out mathematically. Excellent physics text for self-study as well as class work. Vol. 1: Heat, Sound: motion, acceleration, gravitation, conservation of energy, heat engines, rotation, heat, mechanical energy, etc. 211 illus. 407pp. 5⅜ x 8. Vol. 2: Light, Electricity: images, lenses, prisms, magnetism, Ohm's law, dynamos, telegraph, quantum theory, decline of mechanical view of nature, etc. Bibliography. 13 table appendix. Index. 551 illus. 2 color plates. 508pp. 5⅜ x 8.

Vol. 1 S565 Paperbound **$2.00**
Vol. 2 S566 Paperbound **$2.00**
The set **$4.00**

FROM EUCLID TO EDDINGTON: A STUDY OF THE CONCEPTIONS OF THE EXTERNAL WORLD, Sir Edmund Whittaker. A foremost British scientist traces the development of theories of natural philosophy from the western rediscovery of Euclid to Eddington, Einstein, Dirac, etc. The inadequacy of classical physics is contrasted with present day attempts to understand the physical world through relativity, non-Euclidean geometry, space curvature, wave mechanics, etc. 5 major divisions of examination: Space; Time and Movement; the Concepts of Classical Physics; the Concepts of Quantum Mechanics; the Eddington Universe. 212pp. 5⅜ x 8.
T491 Paperbound **$1.35**

THE STORY OF ATOMIC THEORY AND ATOMIC ENERGY, J. G. Feinberg. Wider range of facts on physical theory, cultural implications, than any other similar source. Completely nontechnical. Begins with first atomic theory, 600 B.C., goes through A-bomb, developments to 1959. Avogadro, Rutherford, Bohr, Einstein, radioactive decay, binding energy, radiation danger, future benefits of nuclear power, dozens of other topics, told in lively, related, informal manner. Particular stress on European atomic research. "Deserves special mention . . . authoritative," Saturday Review. Formerly "The Atom Story." New chapter to 1959. Index. 34 illustrations. 251pp. 5⅜ x 8.
T625 Paperbound **$1.45**

THE STRANGE STORY OF THE QUANTUM, AN ACCOUNT FOR THE GENERAL READER OF THE GROWTH OF IDEAS UNDERLYING OUR PRESENT ATOMIC KNOWLEDGE, B. Hoffmann. Presents lucidly and expertly, with barest amount of mathematics, the problems and theories which led to modern quantum physics. Dr. Hoffmann begins with the closing years of the 19th century, when certain trifling discrepancies were noticed, and with illuminating analogies and examples takes you through the brilliant concepts of Planck, Einstein, Pauli, de Broglie, Bohr, Schroedinger, Heisenberg, Dirac, Sommerfeld, Feynman, etc. This edition includes a new, long postscript carrying the story through 1958. "Of the books attempting an account of the history and contents of our modern atomic physics which have come to my attention, this is the best," H. Margenau, Yale University, in "American Journal of Physics." 32 tables and line illustrations. Index. 275pp. 5⅜ x 8.
T518 Paperbound **$1.45**

SPACE AND TIME, Emile Borel. An entirely non-technical introduction to relativity, by world-renowned mathematician, Sorbonne Professor. (Notes on basic mathematics are included separately.) This book has never been surpassed for insight, and extraordinary clarity of thought, as it presents scores of examples, analogies, arguments, illustrations, which explain such topics as: difficulties due to motion; gravitation a force of inertia; geodesic lines; wave-length and difference of phase; x-rays and crystal structure; the special theory of relativity; and much more. Indexes. 4 appendixes. 15 figures. xvi + 243pp. 5⅜ x 8.
T592 Paperbound **$1.45**

THE RESTLESS UNIVERSE, Max Born. New enlarged version of this remarkably readable account by a Nobel laureate. Moving from sub-atomic particles to universe, the author explains in very simple terms the latest theories of wave mechanics. Partial contents: air and its relatives, electrons & ions, waves & particles, electronic structure of the atom, nuclear physics. Nearly 1000 illustrations, including 7 animated sequences. 325pp. 6 x 9.
T412 Paperbound **$2.00**

SOAP BUBBLES, THEIR COLOURS AND THE FORCES WHICH MOULD THEM, C. V. Boys. Only complete edition, half again as much material as any other. Includes Boys' hints on performing his experiments, sources of supply. Dozens of lucid experiments show complexities of liquid films, surface tension, etc. Best treatment ever written. Introduction. 83 illustrations. Color plate. 202pp. 5⅜ x 8.
T542 Paperbound **95¢**

SPINNING TOPS AND GYROSCOPIC MOTION, John Perry. Well-known classic of science still unsurpassed for lucid, accurate, delightful exposition. How quasi-rigidity is induced in flexible and fluid bodies by rapid motions; why gyrostat falls, top rises; nature and effect on climatic conditions of earth's precessional movement; effect of internal fluidity on rotating bodies, etc. Appendixes describe practical uses to which gyroscopes have been put in ships, compasses, monorail transportation. 62 figures. 128pp. 5⅜ x 8.
T416 Paperbound **$1.00**

MATTER & LIGHT, THE NEW PHYSICS, L. de Broglie. Non-technical papers by a Nobel laureate explain electromagnetic theory, relativity, matter, light and radiation, wave mechanics, quantum physics, philosophy of science. Einstein, Planck, Bohr, others explained so easily that no mathematical training is needed for all but 2 of the 21 chapters. Unabridged. Index. 300pp. 5⅜ x 8.
T35 Paperbound **$1.60**

A SURVEY OF PHYSICAL THEORY, Max Planck. One of the greatest scientists of all time, creator of the quantum revolution in physics, writes in non-technical terms of his own discoveries and those of other outstanding creators of modern physics. Planck wrote this book when science had just crossed the threshold of the new physics, and he communicates the excitement felt then as he discusses electromagnetic theories, statistical methods, evolution of the concept of light, a step-by-step description of how he developed his own momentous theory, and many more of the basic ideas behind modern physics. Formerly "A" Survey of Physics." Bibliography. Index. 128pp. 5⅜ x 8.   S650 Paperbound **$1.15**

THE NATURE OF LIGHT AND COLOUR IN THE OPEN AIR, M. Minnaert. Why is falling snow sometimes black? What causes mirages, the fata morgana, multiple suns and moons in the sky? How are shadows formed? Prof. Minnaert of the University of Utrecht answers these and similar questions in optics, light, colour, for non-specialists. Particularly valuable to nature, science students, painters, photographers. Translated by H. M. Kremer-Priest, K. Jay. 202 illustrations, including 42 photos. xvi + 362pp. 5⅜ x 8.   T196 Paperbound **$1.95**

THE STORY OF X-RAYS FROM RONTGEN TO ISOTOPES, A. R. Bleich. Non-technical history of x-rays, their scientific explanation, their applications in medicine, industry, research, and art, and their effect on the individual and his descendants. Includes amusing early reactions to Röntgen's discovery, cancer therapy, detections of art and stamp forgeries, potential risks to patient and operator, etc. Illustrations show x-rays of flower structure, the gall bladder, gears with hidden defects, etc. Original Dover publication. Glossary. Bibliography. Index. 55 photos and figures. xiv + 186pp. 5⅜ x 8.   T662 Paperbound **$1.35**

TEACH YOURSELF ELECTRICITY, C. W. Wilman. Electrical resistance, inductance, capacitance, magnets, chemical effects of current, alternating currents, generators and motors, transformers, rectifiers, much more. 230 questions, answers, worked examples. List of units. 115 illus. 194pp. 6⅞ x 4¼.   Clothbound **$2.00**

TEACH YOURSELF HEAT ENGINES, E. De Ville. Measurement of heat, development of steam and internal combustion engines, efficiency of an engine, compression-ignition engines, production of steam, the ideal engine, much more. 318 exercises, answers, worked examples. Tables. 76 illus. 220pp. 6⅞ x 4¼.   Clothbound **$2.00**

TEACH YOURSELF MECHANICS, P. Abbott. The lever, centre of gravity, parallelogram of force, friction, acceleration, Newton's laws of motion, machines, specific gravity, gas, liquid pressure, much more. 280 problems, solutions. Tables. 163 illus. 271pp. 6⅞ x 4¼.
                          Clothbound **$2.00**

GREAT IDEAS OF MODERN MATHEMATICS: THEIR NATURE AND USE, Jagjit Singh. Reader with only high school math will understand main mathematical ideas of modern physics, astronomy, genetics, psychology, evolution, etc., better than many who use them as tools, but comprehend little of their basic structure. Author uses his wide knowledge of non-mathematical fields in brilliant exposition of differential equations, matrices, group theory, logic, statistics, problems of mathematical foundations, imaginary numbers, vectors, etc. Original publication. 2 appendixes. 2 indexes. 65 illustr. 322pp. 5⅜ x 8.   S587 Paperbound **$1.55**

MATHEMATICS IN ACTION, O. G. Sutton. Everyone with a command of high school algebra will find this book one of the finest possible introductions to the application of mathematics to physical theory. Ballistics, numerical analysis, waves and wavelike phenomena, Fourier series, group concepts, fluid flow and aerodynamics, statistical measures, and meteorology are discussed with unusual clarity. Some calculus and differential equations theory is developed by the author for the reader's help in the more difficult sections. 88 figures. Index. viii + 236pp. 5⅜ x 8.   T440 Clothbound **$3.50**

FREE! All you do is ask for it!

THE FOURTH DIMENSION SIMPLY EXPLAINED, edited by H. P. Manning. 22 essays, originally Scientific American contest entries, that use a minimum of mathematics to explain aspects of 4-dimensional geometry: analogues to 3-dimensional space, 4-dimensional absurdities and curiosities (such as removing the contents of an egg without puncturing its shell), possible measurements and forms, etc. Introduction by the editor. Only book of its sort on a truly elementary level, excellent introduction to advanced works. 82 figures. 251pp. 5⅜ x 8.
                          T711 Paperbound **$1.35**

FAMOUS BRIDGES OF THE WORLD, D. B. Steinman. An up-to-the-minute revised edition of a book that explains the fascinating drama of how the world's great bridges came to be built. The author, designer of the famed Mackinac bridge, discusses bridges from all periods and all parts of the world, explaining their various types of construction, and describing the problems their builders faced. Although primarily for youngsters, this cannot fail to interest readers of all ages. 48 illustrations in the text. 23 photographs. 99pp. 6⅛ x 9¼.
                          T161 Paperbound **$1.00**

CHEMISTRY AND PHYSICAL CHEMISTRY

ORGANIC CHEMISTRY, F. C. Whitmore. The entire subject of organic chemistry for the practic-ing chemist and the advanced student. Storehouse of facts, theories, processes found else-where only in specialized journals. Covers aliphatic compounds (500 pages on the properties and synthetic preparation of hydrocarbons, halides, proteins, ketones, etc.), alicyclic com-pounds, aromatic compounds, heterocyclic compounds, organophosphorus and organometallic compounds. Methods of synthetic preparation analyzed critically throughout. Includes much of biochemical interest. "The scope of this volume is astonishing," INDUSTRIAL AND ENGINEER-ING CHEMISTRY. 12,000-reference index. 2387-item bibliography. Total of x + 1005pp. 5⅜ x 8. Two volume set.
S700 Vol I Paperbound **$2.00**
S701 Vol II Paperbound **$2.00**
The set **$4.00**

THE PRINCIPLES OF ELECTROCHEMISTRY, D. A. MacInnes. Basic equations for almost every subfield of electrochemistry from first principles, referring at all times to the soundest and most recent theories and results; unusually useful as text or as reference. Covers coulometers and Faraday's Law, electrolytic conductance, the Debye-Hueckel method for the theoretical calculation of activity coefficients, concentration cells, standard electrode potentials, thermo-dynamic ionization constants, pH, potentiometric titrations, irreversible phenomena, Planck's equation, and much more. "Excellent treatise," AMERICAN CHEMICAL SOCIETY JOURNAL. "Highly recommended," CHEMICAL AND METALLURGICAL ENGINEERING. 2 Indices. Appendix. 585-item bibliography. 137 figures. 94 tables. ii + 478pp. 5⅝ x 8⅜.
S52 Paperbound **$2.35**

THE CHEMISTRY OF URANIUM: THE ELEMENT, ITS BINARY AND RELATED COMPOUNDS, J. J. Katz and E. Rabinowitch. Vast post-World War II collection and correlation of thousands of AEC reports and published papers in a useful and easily accessible form, still the most complete and up-to-date compilation. Treats "dry uranium chemistry," occurrences, preparation, prop-erties, simple compounds, isotopic composition, extraction from ores, spectra, alloys, etc. Much material available only here. Index. Thousands of evaluated bibliographical references. 324 tables, charts, figures. xxi + 609pp. 5⅜ x 8.
S757 Paperbound **$2.95**

KINETIC THEORY OF LIQUIDS, J. Frenkel. Regarding the kinetic theory of liquids as a gen-eralization and extension of the theory of solid bodies, this volume covers all types of arrangements of solids, thermal displacements of atoms, interstitial atoms and ions, orientational and rotational motion of molecules, and transition between states of matter. Mathematical theory is developed close to the physical subject matter. 216 bibliographical footnotes. 55 figures. xi + 485pp. 5⅜ x 8.
S94 Clothbound **$3.95**
S95 Paperbound **$2.45**

POLAR MOLECULES, Pieter Debye. This work by Nobel laureate Debye offers a complete guide to fundamental electrostatic field relations, polarizability, molecular structure. Partial con-tents: electric intensity, displacement and force, polarization by orientation, molar polariza-tion and molar refraction, halogen-hydrides, polar liquids, ionic saturation, dielectric con-stant, etc. Special chapter considers quantum theory. Indexed. 172pp. 5⅜ x 8.
S64 Paperbound **$1.50**

ELASTICITY, PLASTICITY AND STRUCTURE OF MATTER, R. Houwink. Standard treatise on rheological aspects of different technically important solids such as crystals, resins, textiles, rubber, clay, many others. Investigates general laws for deformations; determines divergences from these laws for certain substances. Covers general physical and mathematical aspects of plasticity, elasticity, viscosity. Detailed examination of deformations, internal structure of matter in relation to elastic and plastic behavior, formation of solid matter from a fluid, conditions for elastic and plastic behavior of matter. Treats glass, asphalt, gutta percha, balata, proteins, baker's dough, lacquers, sulphur, others. 2nd revised, enlarged edition. Extensive revised bibliography in over 500 footnotes. Index. Table of symbols. 214 figures. xviii + 368pp. 6 x 9¼.
S385 Paperbound **$2.45**

THE PHASE RULE AND ITS APPLICATION, Alexander Findlay. Covering chemical phenomena of 1, 2, 3, 4, and multiple component systems, this "standard work on the subject" (NATURE, London), has been completely revised and brought up to date by A. N. Campbell and N. O. Smith. Brand new material has been added on such matters as binary, tertiary liquid equilibria, solid solutions in ternary systems, quinary systems of salts and water. Completely revised to triangular coordinates in ternary systems, clarified graphic repre-sentation, solid models, etc. 9th revised edition. Author, subject indexes. 236 figures. 505 footnotes, mostly bibliographic. xii + 494pp. 5⅜ x 8.
S91 Paperbound **$2.45**

TERNARY SYSTEMS: INTRODUCTION TO THE THEORY OF THREE COMPONENT SYSTEMS, G. Masing. Furnishes detailed discussion of representative types of 3-components systems, both in solid models (particularly metallic alloys) and isothermal models. Discusses mechanical mixture without compounds and without solid solutions; unbroken solid solution series; solid solutions with solubility breaks in two binary systems; iron-silicon-aluminum alloys; allotropic forms of iron in ternary system; other topics. Bibliography. Index. 166 illustrations. 178pp. 5⅝ x 8⅜. **S631 Paperbound $1.45**

THE STORY OF ALCHEMY AND EARLY CHEMISTRY, J. M. Stillman. An authoritative, scholarly work, highly readable, of development of chemical knowledge from 4000 B.C. to downfall of phlogiston theory in late 18th century. Every important figure, many quotations. Brings alive curious, almost incredible history of alchemical beliefs, practices, writings of Arabian Prince Oneeyade, Vincent of Beauvais, Geber, Zosimos, Paracelsus, Vitruvius, scores more. Studies work, thought of Black, Cavendish, Priestley, Van Helmont, Bergman, Lavoisier, Newton, etc. Index. Bibliography. 579pp. 5⅜ x 8. **S628 Paperbound $2.45**

See also: **ATOMIC SPECTRA AND ATOMIC STRUCTURE**, G. Herzberg; **INVESTIGATIONS ON THE THEORY OF THE BROWNIAN MOVEMENT**, A. Einstein; **TREATISE ON THERMODYNAMICS**, M. Planck.

ASTRONOMY AND ASTROPHYSICS

AN ELEMENTARY SURVEY OF CELESTIAL MECHANICS, Y. Ryabov. Elementary exposition of gravitational theory and celestial mechanics. Historical introduction and coverage of basic principles, including: the elliptic, the orbital plane, the 2- and 3-body problems, the discovery of Neptune, planetary rotation, the length of the day, the shapes of galaxies, satellites (detailed treatment of Sputnik I), etc. First American reprinting of successful Russian popular exposition. Elementary algebra and trigonometry helpful, but not necessary; presentation chiefly verbal. Appendix of theorem proofs. 58 figures. 165pp. 5⅜ x 8. **T756 Paperbound $1.25**

THE SKY AND ITS MYSTERIES, E. A. Beet. One of most lucid books on mysteries of universe; deals with astronomy from earliest observations to latest theories of expansion of universe, source of stellar energy, birth of planets, origin of moon craters, possibility of life on other planets. Discusses effects of sunspots on weather; distances, ages of several stars; master plan of universe; methods and tools of astronomers; much more. "Eminently readable book," London Times. Extensive bibliography. Over 50 diagrams. 12 full-page plates, fold-out star map. Introduction. Index, 238pp. 5¼ x 7½. **T627 Clothbound $3.00**

THE REALM OF THE NEBULAE, E. Hubble. One of the great astronomers of our time records his formulation of the concept of "island universes," and its impact on astronomy. Such topics are covered as the velocity-distance relation; classification, nature, distances, general field of nebulae; cosmological theories; nebulae in the neighborhood of the Milky Way. 39 photos of nebulae, nebulae clusters, spectra of nebulae, and velocity distance relations shown by spectrum comparison. "One of the most progressive lines of astronomical research," The Times (London). New introduction by A. Sandage. 55 illustrations. Index. iv + 201pp. 5⅜ x 8. **S455 Paperbound $1.50**

OUT OF THE SKY, H. H. Nininger. A non-technical but comprehensive introduction to "meteoritics", the young science concerned with all aspects of the arrival of matter from outer space. Written by one of the world's experts on meteorites, this work shows how, despite difficulties of observation and sparseness of data, a considerable body of knowledge has arisen. It defines meteors and meteorites; studies fireball clusters and processions, meteorite composition, size, distribution, showers, explosions, origins, craters, and much more. A true connecting link between astronomy and geology. More than 175 photos, 22 other illustrations. References. Bibliography of author's publications on meteorites. Index. viii + 336pp. 5⅜ x 8. **T519 Paperbound $1.85**

SATELLITES AND SCIENTIFIC RESEARCH, D. King-Hele. Non-technical account of the manmade satellites and the discoveries they have yielded up to the spring of 1959. Brings together information hitherto published only in hard-to-get scientific journals. Includes the life history of a typical satellite, methods of tracking, new information on the shape of the earth, zones of radiation, etc. Over 60 diagrams and 6 photographs. Mathematical appendix. Bibliography of over 100 items. Index. xii + 180pp. 5⅜ x 8½. **T703 Clothbound $4.00**

HOW TO MAKE A TELESCOPE, Jean Texereau. Enables the most inexperienced to choose, design, and build an f/6 or f/8 Newtonian type reflecting telescope, with an altazimuth Couder mounting, suitable for lunar, planetary, and stellar observation. A practical step-by-step course covering every operation and every piece of equipment. Basic principles of geometric and physical optics are discussed (though unnecessary to construction), and the merits of reflectors and refractors compared. A thorough discussion of eyepieces, finders, grinding, installation, testing, using the instrument, etc. 241 figures and 38 photos show almost every operation and tool. Potential errors are anticipated as much as possible. Foreword by A. Couder. Bibliography and sources of supply listing. Index. xiii + 191pp. 6¼ x 10. **T464 Clothbound $3.50**

AN INTRODUCTORY TREATISE ON DYNAMICAL ASTRONOMY, H. C. Plummer. Unusually wide connected and concise coverage of nearly every significant branch of dynamical astronomy, stressing basic principles throughout: determination of orbits, planetary theory, lunar theory, precession and nutation, and many of their applications. Hundreds of formulas and theorems worked out completely, important methods thoroughly explained. Covers motion under a central attraction, orbits of double stars and spectroscopic binaries, the libration of the moon, and much more. Index. 8 diagrams. xxi + 343pp. 5⅝ x 8⅜. S689 Paperbound **$2.35**

A COMPENDIUM OF SPHERICAL ASTRONOMY, S. Newcomb. Long a standard collection of basic methods and formulas most useful to the working astronomer, and clear full text for students. Includes the most important common approximations; 40 pages on the method of least squares; general theory of spherical coordinates; parallax; aberration; astronomical refraction; theory of precession; proper motion of the stars; methods of deriving positions of stars; and much more. Index. 9 Appendices of tables, formulas, etc. 36 figures. xviii + 444pp. 5⅜ x 8.
S690 Paperbound **$2.25**

AN INTRODUCTORY TREATISE ON THE LUNAR THEORY, E. W. Brown. Indispensable for all scientists and engineers interested in orbital calculation, satellites, or navigation of space. Only work in English to explain in detail 5 major mathematical approaches to the problem of 3 bodies, those of Laplace, de Pontécoulant, Hansen, Delaunay, and Hill. Covers expressions for mutual attraction, equations of motion, forms of solution, variations of the elements in disturbed motion, the constants and their interpretations, planetary and other disturbing influences, etc. Index. Bibliography. Tables. xvi + 292pp. 5⅝ x 8⅜.
S666 Paperbound **$2.00**

LES METHODES NOUVELLES DE LA MECANIQUE CELESTE, H. Poincaré. Complete text (in French) of one of Poincaré's most important works. This set revolutionized celestial mechanics: first use of integral invariants, first major application of linear differential equations, study of periodic orbits, lunar motion and Jupiter's satellites, three body problem, and many other important topics. "Started a new era . . . so extremely modern that even today few have mastered his weapons," E. T. Bell. Three volumes. Total 1282pp. 6⅛ x 9¼.
Vol. 1. S401 Paperbound **$2.75**
Vol. 2. S402 Paperbound **$2.75**
Vol. 3. S403 Paperbound **$2.75**
The set **$7.50**

SPHERICAL AND PRACTICAL ASTRONOMY, W. Chauvenet. First book in English to apply mathematical techniques to astronomical problems is still standard work. Covers almost entire field, rigorously, with over 300 examples worked out. Vol. 1, spherical astronomy, applications to nautical astronomy; determination of hour angles, parallactic angle for known stars; interpolation; parallax; laws of refraction; predicting eclipses; precession, nutation of fixed stars; etc. Vol. 2, theory, use, of instruments; telescope; measurement of arcs, angles in general; electro-chronograph; sextant, reflecting circles; zenith telescope; etc. 100-page appendix of detailed proof of Gauss' method of least squares. 5th revised edition. Index. 15 plates, 20 tables. 1340pp. 5⅜ x 8. Vol. 1 S618 Paperbound **$2.75**
Vol. 2 S619 Paperbound **$2.75**
The set **$5.50**

THE INTERNAL CONSTITUTION OF THE STARS, Sir A. S. Eddington. Influence of this has been enormous; first detailed exposition of theory of radiative equilibrium for stellar interiors, of all available evidence for existence of diffuse matter in interstellar space. Studies quantum theory, polytropic gas spheres, mass-luminosity relations, variable stars, etc. Discussions of equations paralleled with informal exposition of intimate relationship of astrophysics with great discoveries in atomic physics, radiation. Introduction. Appendix. Index. 421pp. 5⅜ x 8.
S563 Paperbound **$2.25**

ASTRONOMY OF STELLAR ENERGY AND DECAY, Martin Johnson. Middle level treatment of astronomy as interpreted by modern atomic physics. Part One is non-technical, examines physical properties, source of energy, spectroscopy, fluctuating stars, various models and theories, etc. Part Two parallels these topics, providing their mathematical foundation. "Clear, concise, and readily understandable," American Library Assoc. Bibliography. 3 indexes. 29 illustrations. 216pp. 5⅜ x 8. S537 Paperbound **$1.50**

Dover publishes books on art, music, philosophy, literature, languages, history, social sciences, psychology, handcrafts, orientalia, puzzles and entertainments, chess, pets and gardens, books explaining science, intermediate and higher mathematics, mathematical physics, engineering, biological sciences, earth sciences, classics of science, etc. Write to:

Dept. catrr.
Dover Publications, Inc.
180 Varick Street, N. Y. 14, N. Y.